MEMORIES OF LENIN

By the same Author

MEMORIES OF LENIN

VOL. I

FROM 1894 TO 1907

Uniform with this Volume

MEMORIES OF LENIN

by

Nadezhda K. Krupskaya

VOLUME II

NEW YORK
INTERNATIONAL PUBLISHERS

PRINTED AND MADE IN ENGLAND BY
THE GARDEN CITY PRESS LTD., LETCHWORTH, HERTS.

CONTENTS

PREFACE TO VOLUME II

THE second part of the *Memories of Lenin* was written several years after the first, when many other reminiscences and symposiums on Lenin and the second edition of his works had already been published. This has put a definite imprint upon the Memories of the second period of exile. I was able to verify the correctness of my recollections, but on the other hand, the vividness of my memories was diminished to a certain extent. Besides, the period with which these Memories deal (1908-17), was much more complex than the preceding one.

The first period (1893-1907) was the period of the first steps of the Labour Movement in Russia, the struggle for the creation of a Party, the gradual growth of the first revolution—which was directed mainly against tsarism—and the suppression of this revolution. The second period—the years of the second exile—is far more complex. These were years of the summing up of the revolutionary struggle of the first period, years of struggle against reaction and the corrupting influence of this reaction on the Party. These were years of furious struggle against opportunism in all its forms, a struggle to adapt our work to all sorts of conditions without diminishing its revolutionary content. The years of the second exile were the years which marked the approach of the World War, when the opportunism of the Labour Parties brought about the collapse of the Second International, during which it was necessary to hew new paths and, step by step, to lay the foundation for the Third International, when we had to begin the struggle for Socialism under the most trying conditions. In exile all these problems rose up concretely and sharply. Unless these problems are understood it will be impossible to understand how Lenin rose to be the leader of the October Revolution, and of the World Revolution. Leaders are made and developed in the struggle, it is from the struggle that they draw their strength. It is impossible to write the reminiscences of Lenin during the years of exile without linking up every detail of his life with the struggle he carried on during those years.

During the nine years of his second exile, Lenin did not change. He worked as hard and as methodically as ever. As before, he carefully scrutinised every detail and linked up everything into one whole. He was as able as ever to look truth in the face no matter how bitter it was. As before, he hated every form of exploitation and oppression. He was just as devoted to the proletarian cause, to the cause of the toilers. As before, he took their interest to heart and his whole life was subordinated to the interest of this cause. This he did quite unconsciously; he could not live otherwise. He fought just as ardently and resolutely against opportunism and against any attempt to "back out." As before, he would break off relations with his closest friends if he thought they were hampering the movement; and he could approach an opponent of yesterday in a simple and comradely way if the cause required it. He was as blunt and straightforward as ever. He loved the country, the verdant forests, the mountain paths and lakes; but he also loved the noise of a big city, the crowds of workers, his comrades, the movement, the struggle, and life with all its facets. However, watching him closely from day to day, one could observe that he became more reserved and more considerate of people. He became more reflective, and when interrupted in his reverie one seemed to catch a glint of sadness in his eyes. The years of exile were hard to bear and drained much of Lenin's strength. But they made him the fighter the masses needed and the one who led them to victory.

N. KRUPSKAYA.

INTRODUCTION

THE second enforced exile may be divided into three periods:

The first period (1908-11) was the period of the most rabid reaction in Russia. The tsarist government took cruel revenge on the revolutionaries. The prisons were over-crowded; prison conditions were brutal; the infliction of corporal punishment was a common practice; death sentences followed one after another. The illegal organisations were compelled to go deep under ground, but it was not easy to conceal the organisations. During the revolution the character of the membership of the Party had changed; many members had joined who were not familiar with pre-revolutionary work and were not accustomed to the rules of secrecy. On the other hand the tsarist government spared no money for the organisation of espionage and provocation. Its system of espionage was exceedingly well planned, had wide ramifications and even penetrated the central organs of the Party. The government's secret service was excellently organised.

Even the legal organisations, trade unions and the press were systematically persecuted. The government exerted every effort to deprive the masses of the workers of the rights they had won during the revolution. But a return to the past was impossible. The revolution had taught the masses a great deal, and the initiative of the workers again and again found outlets for their activities in every crevice of the police system.

Those were the years of the greatest ideological confusion among the Social-Democrats. Attempts were made to revise the principles of Marxism; new philosophic movements tried to shake the materialistic philosophy upon which the entire Marxian theory is based. The outlook was gloomy in the extreme. Attempts were made to find a way out by concocting a new, subtle religion and giving it a philosophical basis. At the head of this new philosophical school, which opened its doors to every "god seeker" and "god creator," stood Bogdanov supported by Lunacharsky, Bazarov and others. Marx arrived at Marxism by the path of philosophy, through the struggle against idealism. Plekhanov in his time had devoted considerable attention to the enunciation of the materialist philosophy. Lenin studied their works and philosophy generally very intensively while in exile. He could not ignore the significance of this attempt to revise the philosophic basis of Marxism and its relative importance during the years of reaction. And so he came out most strongly in opposition to Bogdanov and his school.

Bogdanov was an opponent not only on the philosophic front. He gathered about him the Otzovists and the Ultimatists.*

The Otzovists maintained that the State Duma had become so reactionary that the Social-Democratic members should be recalled from it. The Ultimatists were of the opinion that an ultimatum should be presented to the Social-Democratic members of the Duma calling upon them to make such speeches in the Duma as would cause them to be ejected. In essence, there was no difference between the Otzovists and the Ultimatists. Among the

* Otzovists—From the Russian word "otozvat," meaning to "recall." Ultimatists—From the word "ultimatum."—Ed.

Ultimatists were Alexinsky,* Marat and others. The Otzovists and Ultimatists were opposed to the Bolsheviks taking part in the work of the trade unions and of the legal organisations. Bolsheviks, they said, must be hard and unyielding. Lenin disagreed with their point of view. He argued that if it were adopted it would mean abstaining from all practical work, isolation from the masses, and failure to organise them for the purpose of fighting for their vital interests. In the period before the 1905 Revolution the Bolsheviks were able to utilise every legal possibility to forge ahead and to lead the masses under the most trying conditions. They began with the struggle for the daily needs of the workers such as demanding that the employers provide hot water for tea, proper ventilation, etc., and from this led the masses, step by step, to the general armed insurrection. The ability to adapt oneself to the most difficult conditions and at the same time to maintain the revolutionary positions—such were the traditions of Leninism. The Otzovists broke with Bolshevik traditions. Hence, the fight against Otzovism was the fight for the tried and tested Bolshevik Leninist tactics.

Finally, these years (1908-11) were years of sharp struggle for the Party and for its illegal organisation.

Naturally, the first to be affected by the spirit of pessimism in the period of reaction were the Mensheviks, who, even before this time had tended to swim with the stream, to tone down revolutionary slogans and had been closely bound up with the liberal bourgeoisie. This pessimistic mood was very strikingly expressed in the effort of a large section of the Mensheviks to dissolve the Party. The liquida-

* Later became a renegade, and after the February Revolution, 1917, circulated a document which was intended to prove that Lenin was in the pay of the Germans.—Ed.

tors, as they were called, maintained that the existence of an illegal party leads to police raids and arrests, and restricts the scope of the labour movement. But in reality, the liquidation of the illegal party would have meant abandoning the independent policy of the proletariat, subduing the revolutionary spirit of the proletarian struggle, and weakening the organisation and the unity of action of the proletariat. The liquidation of the Party would have meant abandoning the principles and tactics of Marx.

Of course, Mensheviks, like Plekhanov, who had done so much for the propagation of Marxism, and for the struggle against opportunism, could not but realise that the moods in favour of dissolving the Party were reactionary, and when propaganda in favour of the liquidation of the Party began to grow into propaganda in favour of repudiating the very principles of Marxism, he completely dissociated himself from the liquidators and formed a group of his own known as the "Party-Mensheviks."

The struggle for the Party which developed helped to clear up a number of organisational questions, and the rank and file of the Party obtained a better understanding of the rôle of the Party and of the duties of its members.

The struggle for the materialist philosophy, for close connection with the masses, for Leninist tactics and for the Party was waged in the conditions and environment of exile.

During the years of reaction, the number of exiles from Russia increased enormously; people fled from the severe persecution of the tsarist régime, their nerves worn and shattered, with no prospects for the future, penniless and without any help from Russia. All this served to give the political struggle exceptional acerbity. Of squabbling and bickering there was more than enough.

Looking back on this period now, after so many years, the issue around which the struggle centred is transparently clear. Now that experience has so definitely proved the correctness of Lenin's policy, this struggle seems to be of little interest to many, but without this struggle the Party would not have been able to develop its work so quickly during the years of the revival of the movement and its path to victory would have been more difficult. The struggle took place when the above-mentioned trends were just developing and was fought between those who, only recently, had been fighting side by side, and to many it seemed that the trouble was due to Lenin's quarrelsomeness, his brusqueness and bad temper. In reality, however, it was a struggle for the very existence of the Party, for a consistent Party policy and for correct tactics. The sharp form the controversy assumed was due to the complicated nature of the questions discussed, and Ilyich frequently presented these questions in a particularly sharp form, otherwise the essence of the question would have remained obscure.

The years 1908 to 1911 were not merely years of sojourn abroad, they were years of intense struggle on the most important front—the front of ideological struggle.

The second period of the second exile (1911-14) was the period of the revival of the movement in Russia. The growth of the strike movement and the shootings in the Lena goldfields which called forth the unanimous protest of the whole of the working class, the development of the labour press, the elections to the Duma and the work of the Social-Democratic members in the Duma—all this gave rise to new forms of Party work, created far wider scope for Party work, made the Party more proletarian in membership and brought it nearer to the masses.

Contacts with Russia rapidly began to improve, and great influence was exercised upon the work in Russia. The Party Conference, held in Prague in January 1912, expelled the liquidators and laid down the organisational principles of the illegal Party. Plekhanov did not join the Bolsheviks.

In 1912 we moved to Cracow. The struggle for the Party and for its consolidation was no longer waged between small groups abroad. In the Cracow period, the Leninist tactics were tested in practice in Russia and proved correct. Lenin became completely absorbed in questions of practical work.

But at the same time that the labour movement was growing in Russia a storm was brewing on the international front. Things began more and more to smack of war, and Ilyich began to ponder over the relationships that would have to be established between the various nations when the impending war was converted into civil war. While living in Cracow, Ilyich had the opportunity of coming into closer contact with the Polish Social-Democrats and to study their point of view on the national question. He persistently combated their mistakes on this question, and more precisely and definitely formulated his own point of view on it. During the Cracow period the Bolsheviks adopted a series of resolutions on the national question which were of great significance.

The third period of the second exile (1914-17) covers the years of the war, when, once again, the whole character of our life abroad underwent a sharp change. This was the period in which international questions assumed decisive importance, in which our

Russian affairs could be interpreted only from the point of view of the international movement.

Another foundation, of much wider dimensions, an international foundation, had now to serve as the base for the movement. Everything that could be done in a neutral country was done to carry on propaganda against the imperialist war and for converting this war into civil war and to lay the foundations for a new International. This work absorbed all Lenin's efforts during the first years of the war (the end of 1914 and the whole of 1915).

Influenced by the events going on around him, new ideas occurred to Lenin. He was drawn to a closer and deeper study of the problems of imperialism, of the character of the war, of the new forms of the state that will arise on the morrow of the victory of the proletariat, of the application of the dialectic method to working-class policy and tactics. We moved from Berne to Zurich where there were better facilities for study. Ilyich gave himself up entirely to writing. He spent whole days in the libraries until news came of the February revolution and we began to make our preparations for departure to Russia.

YEARS OF REACTION

GENEVA
(1908)

ON the evening of our arrival in Geneva, Ilyich wrote a letter to Alexinsky—the Bolshevik deputy in the Second Duma who, together with other Bolshevik deputies had been sentenced to hard labour and who had migrated abroad and was living in Austria at that time—in answer to his letter received in Berlin. A few days later he wrote to Maxim Gorki who had been pressing Ilyich to come to visit him in Italy on the island of Capri.

It was impossible to go to Capri because it was necessary to start work on the publication of *Proletarii*, the illegal central organ of the Party. This had to be done as quickly as possible in order to provide the systematic leadership of the movement in Russia, so essential in those hard times of reaction, through the medium of a central organ. It was impossible to go; but in his letter Ilyich dreamed as it were: "Certainly, it would be important to slip over to Capri!" Then he went on to say: "I think I'd better come to you when you don't have so much work, so that we can lounge about and talk." Ilyich had lived through and thought over so many things in the past few years that he longed for a heart-to-heart talk with Gorki, but he was forced to postpone the trip.

It had not yet been decided whether *Proletarii* was to be published in Geneva or in some other place abroad. We wrote to Austria, to the Austrian Social-Democrat, Adler, and to Joseph (Dzerzhinsky),* who also lived there. Austria was closer to the Russian frontier; in some respects it would have been easier to print the paper there and transportation to Russia would have been easier too. But Ilyich had little hope of being able to organise the publication of the paper anywhere but in Geneva, and so he took the necessary measures for starting work in the latter place. To our surprise, we discovered a type-setting machine in Geneva that belonged to us and had been left over from former days. This reduced expenses and simplified matters.

Comrade Vladimirov, the compositor who set the type for *Vperyod* (*Forward*), the Bolshevik paper published in Geneva before the 1905 revolution, turned up. D. M. Kotlyarenko was placed in charge of general business matters. By February all the comrades who had been sent from Russia to organise the publication of the paper—Lenin, Bogdanov and Innokenty (Dubrovinsky)—had assembled in Geneva.

In a letter dated February 2nd, Vladimir Ilyich wrote to Maxim Gorki: "Everything is ready. We will announce publication in a few days. We have put you down as one of our contributors. Drop me a few lines and let me know whether you will be able to contribute something for the first issues (something like 'Notes on Philistinism' in *Novaya Zhizn* (*New Life*), or extracts from the novel you are now writing, etc.)." As far back as 1894, Lenin, in his book *What the Friends of the People Are and How They Fight Against the Social Democrats*, wrote about bour-

* A prominent Polish Social-Democrat and Bolshevik. After the October revolution, was head of the G.P.U. and later chairman of the Supreme Council of National Economy. Died 1926.—Ed.

geois culture and about the philistinism of the petty-bourgeoisie which he profoundly hated and despised. Hence he was particularly pleased with Gorki's articles on philistinism.

To Lunacharsky, who had gone to live with Gorki at Capri, Ilyich wrote: "Scribble me a line to let me know whether you are properly fixed up and whether you are fit for work again."

The editorial board (Lenin, Bogdanov, Innokenty) sent a letter to Trotsky in Vienna inviting him to contribute to the paper, but Trotsky refused. He did not really want to work with the Bolsheviks, but he did not say so openly; he excused himself on the ground that he was too busy.

The worries about shipping the paper to Russia began. We tried to restore the old contacts. In the past we had shipped our literature to Russia by sea via Marseilles. Ilyich thought that now arrangements could be made to ship the paper via Capri where Gorki lived. He wrote to Maria Fedorovna Andreyeva, Gorki's wife, instructing her to arrange with ships' employees and workers for the shipment of literature to Odessa. He also wrote to Alexinsky asking him to arrange for shipment through Vienna, although he had little hope for success in this quarter. Alexinsky was quite unfitted for such work. We wrote to our "shipping expert," Piatnitsky, now one of the leading workers in the Comintern, who in the past had done excellent work in getting literature across the German border. Piatnitsky was in Russia, and by the time he had succeeded in evading the police, escaping arrest and crossing the frontier to reach us, nearly eight months elapsed. While on the way, he tried to arrange for shipping the paper through Lvov, but was unsuccessful.

He arrived in Geneva in the autumn of 1908. We

decided that he should go back to Leipzig, where he had lived previously, to try to pick up old contacts and organise the shipment of the paper across the German frontier as he had done in the past. Alexinsky decided to come to Geneva. His wife, Tatyana Ivanovna, was to help me with the correspondence with Russia. But these were only plans. As for letters, we waited for them more than we received them.

Soon after we arrived in Geneva an incident occurred in connection with the changing of money. In July 1907 a raid was made on the offices of the State Treasury on Erivan Square in Tiflis. When the revolutionary movement was at its height, and the fight against the autocracy was being waged on an extended front, the Bolsheviks admitted the expediency of making raids, or expropriations as they were called, on the State Treasury. Such a raid was made in Tiflis. The money obtained in the Tiflis raid was handed over to the Bolsheviks for revolutionary purposes. But it was impossible to use the money because it consisted of 500 ruble notes which had to be changed. It was impossible to change the notes in Russia because every bank had received a list of the numbers of the notes and watch was being kept. Reaction was rampant; it was necessary to arrange for the escape of revolutionaries who were being tortured in prison; in order to prevent the movement from dying out it was necessary to establish secret printing shops to print literature, etc. Money was urgently needed. And so a group of comrades organised attempts to change the 500 ruble notes in a number of towns simultaneously. Such an attempt had been made in Geneva only a few days after our arrival. An *agent provocateur* named Zhitomirsky knew about this and took part in it. At that time, of course, no one knew that Zhitomirsky was an *agent provocateur* and everyone had complete confidence in him; but at that time he had already betrayed Comrade Kamo in Berlin. Thanks to Zhitomirsky's treachery Comrade Kamo was caught with a suitcase containing dynamite. He was arrested by the German police and sentenced to a long term of imprisonment. Later, he was handed over to the Russian authorities. This Zhitomirsky warned the police about the attempt that was to be made to change the notes and those engaged in it were arrested. A Lettish comrade, member of the Zurich group, was arrested in Stockholm and Olga Ravich, a member of the Geneva group of our Party, who had recently come from Russia, and Bogdassarian and N. Khodzhamirean were arrested in Munich.

In Geneva, N. A. Semashko* was arrested. A postcard had been sent to one of the arrested men, addressed to his house.

The good Swiss burghers were frightened to death by this incident. The only thing one heard talked about was the Russian "expropriators." They were discussed with horror around the dining-table, in the boarding-house, where Ilyich and I usually dined. When Mikha Tskhakaya, the Caucasian comrade and chairman of the Third Congress of the Party, who lived in Geneva at that time, came to see us for the first time, in his Caucasian costume, his appearance so frightened our landlady, who no doubt thought that he looked the picture of a brigand, that, with a shriek of fright, she slammed the door in his face.

At that time ultra-opportunist views predominated

* After the October Revolution he became Commissar of Public Health.—Ed.

in the Social-Democratic Party of Switzerland and in connection with the arrest of N. A. Semashko, the Swiss Social-Democrats declared that their country was the most democratic in the world, that justice was supreme in their country and that therefore they could not tolerate acts of violence against private property in their territory.

The Russian government demanded extradition of the prisoners. The Swedish Social-Democrats were prepared to intervene, but they demanded that the Zurich group, to which one of the arrested comrades belonged, declare that the lad who was arrested in Stockholm was a Social-Democrat and had lived all the time in Zurich. The Zurich group in which the Mensheviks predominated refused to do this. The Mensheviks also hastened to dissociate themselves from Semashko in the local Berne press, in which they declared that Semashko was not a Social-Democrat and did not represent the Geneva group at the Stuttgart Congress.

The Mensheviks had condemned the Moscow uprising of 1905; they were opposed to everything that might frighten the liberal bourgeoisie. They declared that the fact that the bourgeois intelligentsia deserted the revolution in the time of defeat was due not to the class character of the bourgeois intelligentsia, but to the fact that they were terrified by the methods of struggle employed by the Bolsheviks. They strongly condemned the claim of the Bolsheviks that when the revolutionary struggle was at its height, expropriation was a legitimate method of raising funds for revolutionary purposes. They were of the opinion that the Bolsheviks frightened the liberal bourgeoisie away. Hence the Bolsheviks had to be combatted by fair means or foul.

In a letter dated February 26th, 1908, written to

Plekhanov, P. B. Axelrod unfolded a plan to discredit the Bolsheviks in the eyes of the foreigners, and to use the money-changing incident for this purpose. He proposed that a report be drawn up which should be translated into German and French and sent to the Management Committee (Vorstand) of the Social-Democratic Party of Germany, to Kautsky, Adler, the International Socialist Bureau, to London, etc.

Axelrod's letter, which was published many years later (1926) clearly shows how even at that time the paths of the Bolsheviks and Mensheviks widely diverged.

As representative of the Russian Social-Democratic Labour Party, Vladimir Ilyich sent an official statement to the International Socialist Bureau concerning the arrest of N. A. Semashko. He also wrote to Gorki saying that if he knew Semashko from Nizhni personally he ought to defend him in the Swiss press. Semashko was soon released.

After the revolution, we found it difficult to get accustomed to life in exile again. Vladimir Ilyich spent his days in the library, but in the evenings we did not know what to do with ourselves. We did not feel like sitting in the cold, cheerless room we had rented; we longed to be among people, and every evening we would go to the cinema or to the theatre, although we rarely stayed to the end, but usually left in the middle of the performance and would go wandering somewhere, most often to the lake.

At last, in February, the first issue of *Proletarii* was published in Geneva (No. 21). Vladimir Ilyich's first article in it is characteristic. He wrote:

"We were able to work for long years before the Revolution. It is not for nothing that it was said that we are as hard as granite. The Social-Democrats have built up a proletarian party that will not lose heart at the failure of the first military attack, will not lose its head and will not be drawn into adventurism. This Party is marching towards Socialism without tying its faith to the outcome of this or that period of bourgeois revolutions. This is precisely why it is free from the weaknesses of the bourgeois revolutions. And this proletarian Party is marching to victory."

These words expressed the thoughts that dominated the whole life of Vladimir Ilyich at that time. During the moment of defeat he dreamed of great proletarian victories. He talked about this during our evening walks on the shores of Lake Geneva.

Comrade Adoratsky,* who was banished from Russia in 1906, and went back at the beginning of 1908, was still in Geneva when we arrived there. He recalls the conversation we had with Ilyich on the character of the next revolution in Russia and that Ilyich expressed the view that this revolution would undoubtedly place power in the hands of the proletariat. Comrade Adoratsky's reminiscences confirm the spirit which pervaded the article quoted above and everything else that Lenin said at that time. Ilyich did not doubt for a single moment that the defeat of the proletariat was only temporary.

Comrade Adoratsky also recalls that Vladimir Ilyich made him write a detailed account of the events of 1905 and particularly on the lessons that were to be drawn from the questions concerning the arming of the workers, the organisation of fighting detachments, the organisation of insurrection and seizing power. Vladimir Ilyich thought it was extremely necessary to study very carefully the experiences of the revolution because, as he said, this experi-

* Now head of the Marx-Engels-Lenin Institute in Moscow.—Ed.

ence would be very useful in the future. He would seize upon every one who had taken part in the recent struggle and hold long conversations with them. In his opinion, the task of the Russian working class was: "To safeguard the traditions of the revolutionary struggle which the intelligentsia and the petty bourgeoisie had hastened to renounce; to develop and to strengthen these traditions; to inculcate them into the minds of the broad masses of the people; to carry them over to the next inevitable rise of the democratic movement." "The workers themselves," he wrote, "are spontaneously following precisely this line. They fought in the great October and December battles too passionately; they saw only too clearly that they can change their conditions *only* by means of this direct revolutionary struggle. They now say, or at least they all feel what that textile worker said who wrote in a letter to his trade union paper: 'The employers have taken back all our gains; the foremen are tormenting us as they did before; *but wait*; 1905 *will come again!*' "

"Wait; 1905 will come again. That is how a worker looks at things. To the workers the year of struggle was an example of *what should be done*. To the intelligentsia and to the renegade middle class, this was a 'mad year,' it was an example of *what should not be done*. To the proletariat, the study and critical analysis of the experiences of the revolution meant learning to apply the methods of struggle employed at that time *more successfully*; to convert this very October strike movement and December armed struggle into a broader, more concentrated, more class-conscious struggle."

Ilyich pictured the years ahead as years of preparation for a new attack.

It was necessary to take advantage of the "respite"

in the revolutionary struggle in order to deepen its content still more.

First of all, it was necessary to work out the line of struggle that was to be pursued in the new conditions of reaction that prevailed. It was necessary to think out the means by which, while keeping the Party underground, it would be possible at the same time to enable it to act openly, to keep the possibility of speaking to the broad masses of workers and peasants from the floor of the Duma. Ilyich realised that many of the Bolsheviks, the so-called Otzovists, were trying to simplify the problem; they wanted at all cost to cling to the forms of struggle that were expedient when the revolution was at its height; but by doing so they were actually deserting the struggle in the face of the difficult conditions of reaction, deserting in the face of the difficulties of adapting the work to the new conditions. Ilyich defined the Otzovists as Left-Liquidators. The most outspoken Otzovist was Alexinsky. Soon after his return to Geneva, relations between him and Ilyich became strained. Ilyich had to deal with him in connection with a whole series of questions and he was more than ever repelled by the cock-sure narrow-mindedness of this man. Alexinsky was not in the least concerned with using the Duma, even in the conditions of reaction, as a means of maintaining contact with the broad masses and peasants. Since the Second Duma had been dissolved, he would not be able to speak there any more and so it did not concern him; that was the attitude he took. On the background of Geneva, the egotistical hooliganism of this person seemed to stand out in great relief and nakedness and yet at that time he was still regarded as a Bolshevik.

I recall the following incident: I was walking along the Rue Carouge one day (for years and years this street had been the centre where Russian exiles gathered) and I saw two members of the *Bund* standing in the middle of the side-walk, looking forlorn. They were both members of a committee of which Alexinsky was also a member that was to edit the report of the London Congress (this report was first published in Geneva in 1908). They informed me that a dispute had begun over some formulation or other, and that Alexinsky began to shout at them, grabbed all the reports from the table and ran away. I looked around and in the distance I saw the short figure of Alexinsky walking very briskly, his head proudly raised, with a thick folder of papers under his arm, disappearing around the corner. It was not even funny.

But it was not a matter of Alexinsky alone. It was obvious that the former solidarity of the Bolshevik fraction was gone, that a split was approaching and first of all a split with Bogdanov.

In Russia, a volume entitled *Outlines of the Philosophy of Marxism* appeared containing essays by Bogdanov, Lunacharsky, Bazarov, Suvorov, Berman, Yushkevich and Helfand. The aim of these essays was to revise the materialist philosophy, to revise Marx's materialist conception of the development of humanity and the conception of the class struggle.

The new philosophy opened the doors to every type of mysticism. During the years of reaction when pessimism was rife among the intelligentsia, the soil was particularly ripe for the spread of revisionism. Obviously, the split was inevitable.

Ilyich was always interested in questions of philosophy. He studied philosophy closely while in exile and knew very well the opinions of Marx, Engels and Plekhanov. He had studied Hegel, Feuerbach and Kant. While still in exile in Siberia he had heated controversies with comrades who were inclined towards Kant, he followed up what was written on the subject of philosophy in the *Neue Zeit* and generally speaking was well grounded in philosophy.

In his letter to Gorki, dated February 25th, Ilyich told the story of his differences with Bogdanov. While still in exile Ilyich had read Bogdanov's book, *The Fundamental Elements of the Historical Conception of Nature*, but the position then held by Bogdanov was merely a transitory one to his later philosophic views. In 1903, when Ilyich and Plekhanov worked together, the latter more than once railed against Bogdanov for his philosophic opinions. In 1904 Bogdanov's book, *Empiriomonism*, appeared, and Ilyich flatly declared to Bogdanov that he considered Plekhanov's views right and not Bogdanov's. In his letter to Gorki, Ilyich wrote as follows:

"In the summer and autumn of 1904, Bogdanov and I arrived at a complete agreement as Bolsheviks, and we concluded a tacit *bloc* by which philosophy was tacitly agreed to be a neutral subject. This *bloc* was maintained during the entire period of the revolution and enabled us jointly to carry out the tactics of revolutionary Social-democracy, i.e. Bolshevism which, I am profoundly convinced, were the only correct tactics to adopt.

"When the revolution was at its height, we had little time for philosophy. While in prison, in the beginning of 1906, Bogdanov wrote something else, I think it was Part III of his *Empiriomonism*. In the summer of 1906 he presented me with a copy of this, and I began to study it closely. After having read it, I became unusually annoyed and angry. It became clearer to me than ever that he was taking an exceedingly wrong non-Marxian line. I then wrote to him a 'love-letter'—a letter on philosophy that took up three notebooks. I made it clear to him, that, of course, I was just a *rank-and-file Marxist* in the field of philosophy, but that it was precisely his clear, popularly and excellently written works that completely convinced me that he was wrong and that Plekhanov was right. I showed my notebooks to several friends (Lunacharsky among them) and thought of publishing them with a title: *The Opinions of a Rank-and-File Marxist on Philosophy*, but for some reason or another, I did not do so. Now I am sorry I did not publish them immediately.

"Now the *Outlines of the Philosophy of Marxism* have appeared. I have read all the essays in this volume, except the one by Suvorov (I am reading that now) and every essay made me furious. I would rather be quartered than agree to contribute to a publication or be a member of a group which propagated ideas like those.

"I was again drawn to the *Opinions of a Rank-and-File Marxist on Philosophy* and I began to write. While reading the *Outlines* I wrote to Alexander Alexandrovich (Bogdanov), giving him my impressions, of course, straight from the shoulder."

That is how Vladimir Ilyich described this affair to Gorki.

By the time the first number of *Proletarii* published abroad appeared (February 13th, 1908), the relations between Ilyich and Bogdanov had become extremely strained.

At the end of March Ilyich still considered that philosophical disputes could and should be separated from the political groupings in the Bolshevik fraction. He was of the opinion that philosophical disputes in the fraction would reveal better than anything else that it is impossible to put Bolshevism on the same level as Bogdanov's philosophy.

However, it was becoming clearer every day that the Bolshevik fraction would soon split.

During this difficult period Ilyich became particularly friendly with Innokenty (Dubrovinsky). Until 1905 we had known Innokenty only from hearsay. "Dyadenka" (Lydia Mikhailovna Knipovich) who had met him while in exile in Astrakhan, praised him very highly. He was also praised by the Samarians (the Krzhizhanovskys), but we had never met him nor had we corresponded with him. Only once, after the Second Congress of the Party when the squabble with the Mensheviks flared up, did we receive a letter from him in which he urged the importance of preserving the unity of the Party. Later he became a member of the Conciliatory Central Committee and was arrested together with other members of the Central Committee at Leonid Andreev's flat.

In 1905 Ilyich saw Innokenty at work. He saw how completely devoted Innokenty was to the revolutionary cause, how he undertook the most dangerous and difficult tasks. The latter explains why Innokenty was never able to be present at Party Congresses; he would invariably get arrested before the Congress was held. Ilyich saw how resolute Innokenty was in the struggle—he had taken part in the Moscow uprising and was in Kronstadt during the uprising there. Innokenty was not a literary man. He would speak at meetings of workers in the factories and his speeches inspired the workers in their struggle. But no one wrote the speeches down, of course. Ilyich prized Innokenty greatly for his fervent devotion to the cause and was very glad when he arrived in Geneva. They had much in common and this drew them together. Both of them attached great importance to the Party and both were of the opinion that a determined struggle had to

be waged against the liquidators who argued that
the illegal Party ought to be dissolved because it
only hindered the work. Both of them prized Plekhanov very highly and were glad that the latter had
not joined the liquidators. Both were of the opinion
that Plekhanov was right in the field of philosophy,
that it was absolutely necessary to break away from
Bogdanov and that the struggle on the philosophic
front had now acquired special significance. Ilyich
saw that no one understood his trend of thought so
well as Innokenty did. Innokenty would come to
dine with us and after dinner they would discuss
plans for work and the situation that had arisen. In
the evenings they would meet in the Café Landold
and continue their discussions there. Ilyich infected
Innokenty with his "philosophic intoxication" as he
called it. All this drew them very closely together.
At that time Ilyich became very greatly attached
to Innokenty. This was a very difficult period. In
Russia the organisation was falling to pieces. The
police, with the aid of *agents provocateurs*, caught the
most prominent Party workers. It became impossible to organise big meetings and conferences.
It was not an easy matter for people who only
recently had been prominent in the eyes of the public
to go underground. In the spring (April-May)
Kamenev and Varsky (a Polish Social-Democrat
and intimate friend of Dzerzhinsky, Tyshka and
Rosa Luxemburg) were arrested in the street; a
few days later Zinoviev and finally, N. A. Rozhkov
(a Bolshevik, member of the Central Committee)
were arrested. The masses withdrew into their shell
as it were. They wanted to think over everything
that had occurred; everybody had become tired of
general agitation, it no longer satisfied anyone.
People readily joined study circles, but there was no

one to lead them. This situation created a favourable environment for the growth of Otzovism. The fighting detachments, being left without the leadership of the Party organisation and acting not in connection with the mass struggle but separately from it, became demoralised, and Innokenty had to disentangle more than one complicated case which arose as a consequence.

In order to try and reach an understanding, Gorki invited Vladimir Ilyich to come to Capri, where Bogdanov, Bazarov and others lived at that time, But Ilyich would not go, for he felt that no understanding was possible. In his letter to Gorki of April 16th, he wrote as follows:

"It would be useless and harmful for me to go: *I cannot and will not have anything to do* with people who have set out to propagate unity between scientific socialism and religion. There is no use arguing and it is absurd to upset oneself for nothing."

However, yielding to Gorki's entreaties, Ilyich did go to Capri in May, but he stayed there only a few days. Of course, no conciliation with Bogdanov's philosophical views took place. Afterwards, Ilyich recalled how he had said to Bogdanov and Bazarov; —we will simply have to separate for two or three years,—and that Maria Fedorovna, Gorki's wife, laughingly called him to order.

There was a big crowd at Gorki's place, much noise and bustle. Many played chess, others went boating. Ilyich said very little about this trip. He spoke mostly about the beauty of the scene and the quality of the local wine, but he was reticent about the discussion on the big questions that took place there. It was too painful a subject with him to talk about.

Ilyich again became immersed in the study of philosophy.

c

This is how Vladimir Ilyich describes the situation that prevailed at that time in a letter he wrote the summer of 1908 to Vorovsky, a comrade with whom he had worked on the *Vperyod* and also during the revolution in 1905. Vorovsky lived in Odessa at that time.

"Dear friend: Thanks for your letter. Both your 'suspicions' are wrong. I was not irritable, but the situation is a difficult one. A rupture with Bogdanov is inevitable. The real reason is that he has taken offence at the sharp criticism that was levelled at his philosophical views at lectures (not at meetings of the editorial board). Now Bogdanov is deliberately seeking for points of difference. He and Alexinsky, who is very quarrelsome and with whom I have been obliged to break off all connections, have invented the boycott.* . . . They are preparing for a split on empiriomonistic-boycott grounds. The thing will soon flare up. A fight at the next conference is inevitable. A split is quite probable. If the line of the 'Left' and of true 'boycottism' prevails, I will leave the fraction immediately. I asked you to come because I thought that your speedy arrival would help us to ease the situation. We absolutely count upon your coming in August (new style) as a delegate to the conference. You must plan your work in such a way that you will be able to go abroad. We will send money to all the Bolsheviks for the journey. To the local organisations give the slogan; Give mandates only to local and genuine workers. We beg you to write for our paper. We can now pay for articles and will pay regularly.—Sincerely yours,

" Perhaps you know a publisher who would undertake to publish the book on philosophy that I will write."

* Boycott of the Duma.—Ed.

At this time, the Bolsheviks were fairly well supplied with funds. Young Nickolai Pavlovich Schmidt, a nephew of Morozov* and owner of a furniture factory in the Presnya district of Moscow, came over to the side of the workers in 1905 and joined the Bolsheviks. He provided the money to found *Novaya Zhizn* and also provided money for the purpose of procuring arms. He became intimate with the workers and was one of their best friends. The police called Schmidt's factory a "devil's nest." The factory played an important part during the Moscow uprising. Nikolai Pavlovich was arrested. In prison he was subjected to every kind of torture. The police took him to see what had been done to his factory; they took him to see the murdered workers and finally they murdered him in prison. Before he died, he succeeded in informing his friends outside that he was leaving his property to the Bolsheviks.

Elizaveta Pavlovna Schmidt, Nikolai Pavlovich's younger sister, inherited part of her brother's estate, and she, too, decided to give it to the Bolsheviks. But she was not yet of age and in order that she might be able to dispose of her money as she wished, it was decided to arrange a fictitious marriage. Elizaveta Pavlovna went through a form of marriage with Comrade Ignatyev, a member of the fighting detachment who managed to retain his legality, and being his wife officially, she was able, with the consent of her husband, to do what she liked with her legacy. But the marriage was really a fictitious one. Elizaveta Pavlovna was actually the wife of another Bolshevik, Victor Taratuta. The official marriage enabled her to obtain the legacy immediately and the money was handed over to the Bolsheviks. This

* A textile magnate.—Ed.

is why Ilyich was so certain that *Proletarii* would pay for articles, and that delegates would get money for their travelling expenses to the conference.

In the summer, Victor Taratuta came to Geneva. He assisted in business matters and carried on the correspondence with other centres abroad in the capacity of secretary of the Foreign Bureau of the Central Committee.

Gradually, contacts with Russia were established; correspondence was resumed. Nevertheless, I still had plenty of time on my hands. It seemed that we would have to stay abroad for a long time and so I decided to learn French thoroughly in order to be able to take part in the work of the local Social-Democratic Party. I took the French language course that was organised for foreigners at the Geneva University. I studied the methods of foreign teachers and I not only learned the French language, but also acquired the Swiss ability to work intensely and conscientiously.

Fatigued from work on his book on philosophy, Ilyich would take my French grammars and books on the history of the language and on the study of the peculiarities of the French language, and would lie in bed and read them for hours until his nerves —wrought up by the philosophic disputes—were calmed.

I also began to study the system of education in Geneva, and I realised for the first time what a bourgeois "elementary" school was. I saw how, in excellent buildings, fitted with large, light windows, the children of workers were educated to become docile slaves and observed that in one and the same classroom the teachers would beat and box the ears of workers' children, but never punish the children of the rich. I saw how every independent thought of a child was stifled; learning by rote, predominated over everything and the worship of the power of wealth was inculcated in the children. I never imagined that anything of the kind could take place in a democratic country. I would give Ilyich my impressions in detail. He would listen very attentively.

During the first period of exile, until 1905, Ilyich's observations of life abroad were concentrated mainly on the labour movement. He was particularly interested in labour meetings, demonstrations, etc. Such meetings never took place in Russia before Ilyich went abroad for the first time in 1901. After the revolution in 1905, after having experienced the tremendous upsurge of the labour movement in Russia, the struggles of the Party, the experience of the Duma, and particularly after soviets of workers' deputies had arisen, he not only became interested in the Labour movement abroad, but also, and particularly, in what a bourgeois-democratic republic really was like; what rôle the masses of the workers played in it; how great was the influence of the workers in it, and how great the influence of other parties.

I recalled the half-amazed and half-contemptuous tones in which Ilyich repeated the words of the speech delivered by a Swiss member of Parliament who (in connection with Semashko's arrest) had said that their republic had existed for hundreds of years, and that it could not permit the violation of the rights of property.

The fight for a democratic republic was a point in our programme at that time. Ilyich now realised with particular clarity that a bourgeois democratic republic was perhaps a more subtle instrument than tsarism, but nevertheless an instrument for enslaving the toiling masses. In a democratic republic the authorities do all in their power to imbue the whole of social life with the bourgois spirit.

It seems to me that had Ilyich not lived through the 1905 revolution and the second period of exile, he would not have been able to write his book, *State and Revolution.*

The discussions which had started on questions of philosophy called for the speedy publication of the book on philosophy which Ilyich had begun to write. He needed some material which he could not get in Geneva. Moreover, the bickering and squabbling that was such a marked feature of life in exile, greatly hampered his work. He decided therefore to go to London and work in the British Museum and to finish his book there.

While Lenin was away, Lunacharsky was announced to deliver a lecture in Geneva. Innokenty attended the lecture and took part in the debate that followed. Ilyich had sent him an outline of his speech to which he, Innokenty, had made certain alterations. He was very nervous before the day the lecture was to take place and would sit in our house day after day surrounded by books, and copying excerpts. He made a very good speech, however, and declared in his own name and in that of Lenin that Bolshevism had nothing in common with Bogdanov's philosophical trend (empiriomonism), and that he and Lenin adhered to dialectic materialism and sided with Plekhanov.

Although Lunacharsky delivered the lecture the principle advocate of empirio-criticism at the meeting was Bogdanov and he attacked Innokenty very bitterly. He knew Innokenty very well; he knew that Innokenty stood for an open, straight fight on the philosophical front and knowing how strongly he was imbued with the sense of revolutionary honour, in attacking him, Bogdanov tried to wound him there. Referring to the lecturer, Bogdanov in his speech said: "A knight came forth, bearing a garland of roses; but he was stabbed in the back." This nasty cut did not disturb Innokenty in the least. When Ilyich returned from London he gave him a detailed account of the debate.

Ilyich was pleased with his visit to London. He had managed to collect the materials he required and to work it up. On August 24th, soon after Lenin's return, the meeting of the Central Committee of the Party took place. At this meeting it was decided to hasten the convocation of the Party Conference. Innokenty went to Russia in order to make the necessary preparations. By that time, liquidationism, which had spread to wide sections of the Mensheviks, had already become clearly manifested and began to go strong. The liquidators wanted to dissolve the Party and its illegal organisation, which in their opinion only lead to arrests. They wanted to confine the activities of the Party to purely legal work in trade unions, benefit societies, etc. In the conditions of reaction that then prevailed, this would have meant abandoning all revolutionary activity, abandoning the leadership, the surrender of all positions. On the other hand, in the ranks of the Bolshevik fraction the Ultimatists and Otzovists went to the other extreme; they not only objected to the Party working in the Duma, but also to working in cultural and educational organisations, in clubs, schools, legal trade unions, workers' insurance societies, etc. They completely abandoned work among the broad masses and ceased to lead them.

Innokenty and Ilyich very often discussed the necessity of combining Party leadership (for the preservation of which it was necessary at all costs to

preserve the illegal organisation) with extensive
work among the masses. The immediate task ahead
was to prepare for the Party Conference. It was
agreed that during the campaign for the election of
delegates to the conference extensive agitation
be carried on against the liquidators on the Right
and the Left. Innokenty went to Russia to carry out
this plan. He settled in St. Petersburg where he
organised the work of the Committee of Five of the
Central Committee, consisting of himself, Meshkovsky (Goldenberg) the Menshevik M. I. Broido,
the representative of the Bund and a Lettish representative. Innokenty organised a bureau of which
Golubkov, who later acted as a delegate to the
Central Committee of the Party Conference, was a
member. Innokenty himself did not succeed in
getting to the conference, which took place in
December 1908. About two weeks before the conference was to take place, he was arrested at the
Warsaw Railway station as he was booking his ticket
to go abroad and was exiled to the Vologda Province.

The police proved to be very well informed about
Innokenty's journey to Russia, and no doubt it was
Zhitomirsky who kept them informed. Moreover,
"Lucy," the wife of Serov, a member of the Second
Duma, was brought in to help in the work of the
Bureau of the Central Committee which Innokenty
had organised. Soon after it was discovered that
"Lucy" was an *agent provocateur*.

Ilyich completed his book on philosophy in September, after Innokenty left for Russia. It was
published much later—in May, 1909.

We had completely settled down in Geneva.

My mother arrived and we set up our little household—we rented a small apartment and began
housekeeping. On the surface, our life seemed to be

running smoothly. Maria Ilyinishna* arrived from Russia; other comrades also began to arrive. I remember that Comrade Skrypnik,† who at that time was studying the co-operative movement, also arrived. I accompanied Comrade Skrypnik, in the capacity of interpreter, on visits to the Swiss deputy, Sigg (a terrible opportunist) to discuss the co-operative movement, but the results of these interviews were very meagre, for Sigg and Skrypnik approached the question from entirely different angles. Skrypnik's approach was that of a revolutionary; Sigg, however, regarded the movement as nothing more than well-organised "shopkeeping."

Zinoviev and Lilina arrived from Russia. Lilina gave birth to a son, and she and Zinoviev settled down in their little household. Kamenev and his family arrived. After St. Petersburg, life in this small, quiet, petty-bourgeois town of Geneva seemed awfully dull. We all longed to move to some big centre. The Mensheviks and the Socialist-Revolutionaries had already moved to Paris. Ilyich hesitated. In Geneva, he said, the cost of living was not so high, and there were better facilities for studying there. Finally, Lyadov and Zhitomirsky arrived from Paris and began to persuade us to go there. They advanced a number of arguments in support of this: 1. It would be possible to take part in the French movement; 2. Paris is a large city and there would be less spying; the latter argument convinced Ilyich. In the late autumn we moved to Paris.

In Paris we spent the most trying years of exile. Ilyich always looked back upon them with regret. Time and again he would say: "What the devil made

* Lenin's sister.—Ed.
† Now Commissar of Education in the Ukraine Soviet Republic.—Ed.

us go to Paris?" It was not the devil, but the necesity for beginning the struggle for Marxism, for Leninism, for the Party, in the very centre of Russian exile life. In those years of reaction, that centre was Paris.

PARIS

(1909-10)

WE started out for Paris in the middle of December. On the 21st, a Party Conference was to take place with the Mensheviks and Vladimir Ilyich was completely absorbed with this. It was necessary to appraise the situation correctly, to straighten out the Party line, to see that the Party remained a class party, the vanguard which even during the most trying times would not become isolated from the rank and file, from the masses, that would help them to overcome all difficulties and organise them for fresh battles. It was necessary to check the liquidators. Contacts with the organisation in Russia were bad. The conference could not hope for considerable support from the organisations in Russia (the only delegates to come from Russia were two comrades from Moscow; Baturin came from the Urals and on the second day Poletayev, a member of the Third Duma, came from St. Petersburg). The Otzovists organised themselves in a separate group and were very excited. Before the Party Conference was opened, the Mensheviks called a conference of their groups abroad in Basle at which a number of splitting resolutions were passed. The atmosphere was becoming very tense.

Vladimir Ilyich took only a very remote interest in the efforts we were making to fix up our new quarters. He had more important things to think about. We rented an apartment on the outskirts of the city

on the Rue Bonier, near the fortifications, a street
adjoining the Avenue d'Orléans not far from the
Parc Montsouris. The apartment was light and
spacious and even had mirrors over the fireplaces.
(This was a special feature of the new houses.)
There was a room for my mother, one for Maria
Ilyinishna who had arrived in Paris, one for Vladimir
Ilyich and myself and a living room. But this rather
luxurious apartment did not at all fit in with our
mode of life and the "furniture" we brought from
Geneva. The contempt with which the *concierge*
looked upon our white deal tables, common chairs
and stools was worth seeing. In our "parlour" we
had only a couple of chairs and a small table. It
was not cosy by any means.

The household cares immediately fell to my lot. In
Geneva household affairs were much simpler; here
there seemed to be a lot of red tape about everything.
In order to get the gas connected we had to go three
times to a place in the centre of the city in order to
get the necessary certificate. Bureaucracy is rampant in France. In order to be able to borrow books
from a library, the landlord had to act as guarantor,
and he, judging us by our poor furniture, hesitated
to do so. At first we had a lot of trouble in keeping
house. I was a poor housekeeper; Vladimir Ilyich
and Innokenty were of a different opinion, but people
who are accustomed to real household management
were exceedingly critical of my simple methods.

Life was full of turmoil and bustle in Paris. At
that time Russian exiles were drawn to Paris from
all parts. During this year Ilyich spent little time at
home. Our people would sit in the cafés until late
in the night, Taratuta particularly liked to frequent
the cafés. Little by little, others were drawn into
this habit.

The Party Conference took place in December. After heated debates we managed to adopt a common policy. The *Sotsial-Demokrat* was to become the organ of the Party as a whole. At the meeting of the Central Committee which was held after the Conference, a new editorial board was appointed consisting of Lenin, Zinoviev, Kamenev, Martov and Markhlevsky. Eight issues of the paper were published during the year. Martov was the only Menshevik on the board and often he would forget his Menshevism. I remember that once Vladimir Ilyich remarked with satisfaction that it was a pleasure to work with Martov, and that he was an exceedingly talented journalist. But this was only until Dan arrived.

Within the Bolshevik fraction, however, the relations with the Otzovists became more and more strained, the latter were very aggressive in their opposition and at the end of February relations were completely broken off with them. For three years before the rupture we had been working hand in hand with Bogdanov and his followers—we did not merely work, but fought side by side. Fighting side by side makes people more intimate than anything else in the world. Besides, no one could imbue others with enthusiasm for ideals, infect them with his ardour and at the same time bring out the best in them as Vladimir Ilyich could. Every comrade working with Ilyich seemed, as it were, to be possessed of a part of him. Perhaps that is why they felt so closely drawn to him. The conflict within the fraction was nerve-wracking. I remember once Ilyich came home after a heated debate with the Otzovists. I could hardly recognise him, his face was so drawn and he could barely speak. We decided that he must take a week's holiday at Nice to get the sun and be away from the noise and strife. He went and came back much the better for it.

It was very difficult to study in Paris. The "Bibliothèque Nationale" was far from where we lived. Vladimir Ilyich would generally cycle there, but riding a bicycle in Paris was not what it was in the suburbs of Geneva. It entailed much effort. Ilyich would get very tired from these rides. The library closed at lunch time. Then there was a lot of bother in getting books from the library. Ilyich railed against the library and against Paris. I wrote to a French professor who in the summer had conducted French courses in Geneva asking him to recommend other good libraries. I received an answer immediately with the necessary information. Ilyich made the rounds of all the libraries recommended, but could not find a suitable one. In the end his bicycle was stolen. He used to leave it on the staircase at the house adjoining the " Bibliothèque Nationale," and paid the *concierge* ten centimes a day for this. When the bicycle was stolen the *concierge* declared that she had not undertaken to watch the bicycle, but merely to allow Ilyich to put it up under the staircase.

One had to be very careful in riding a bicycle in Paris and in the suburbs. Once on his way to Juvissy, Ilyich collided with an automobile. He barely managed to jump clear but the bicycle was smashed.

Innokenty, who had escaped from Solvychegodsk, arrived. Zhitomirsky very kindly invited him to live with him. Innokenty arrived very sick. On his way to exile the iron fetters which he wore had so chafed the flesh of his legs that deep wounds were caused. Our doctors examined Innokenty's legs and said a lot of wise things about it, but could do nothing.

Ilyich went to consult the French professor Dubouchier, an excellent surgeon who had worked in Odessa during the 1905 revolution. Ilyich was accompanied by Natasha Hopner who had known Dubouchier in Odessa. When Dubouchier heard the queer things our doctors had told Innokenty he burst out laughing and said: "Your physician comrades may be very good revolutionaries, but as doctors they are jackasses!" Ilyich roared with laughter, and on many occasions afterwards repeated the story. However, Innokenty had to have medical treatment for a long time.

Ilyich was very glad that Innokenty had arrived. They were both happy that Plekhanov was beginning to dissociate himself from the liquidators. He had already announced that he was leaving the editorial board of *Golos Sotsial Demokrata* (*The Voice of the Social-Democrats*), which the liquidators had controlled since 1908. Later on, he withdrew his resignation, but his relations with the liquidators were becoming more strained and on May 26th, 1909, when the first volume of the Menshevik symposium, *The Social Movement in Russia at the Beginning of the Twentieth Century* appeared, which contained an article by Portresov denying the leading rôle of the proletariat in the bourgeois democratic revolution, Plekhanov definitely resigned from the editorial board of *Golos Sotsial Demokrata*. Both Ilyich and Innokenty still hoped that joint work with Plekhanov would be possible. The younger generation did not feel toward Plekhanov the same way as the older generation of Marxists in whose lives Plekhanov had played a decisive rôle. Ilyich and Innokenty took the struggle on the philosophic front very much to heart, for both regarded philosophy as a weapon in the struggle. They were of the opinion that philosophy was organically linked up with the question of evaluating all phenomena from the point of view of dialectic materialism, with the questions of the practical struggle in every field. Ilyich wrote to Anna Ilyinishna asking her to hurry the publication of his book. It was proposed to call an enlarged meeting* of the editorial board of *Proletarii* at which the question was to be raised of completely breaking away from the Otzovists. "The situation is a sad one here," Vladimir Ilyich wrote to his sister Anna Ilyinishna on May 26th, "Spaltung (a split) is inevitable; I hope that in about a month and a half I shall be able to give you an exact account of it."

In May, Ilyich's book *Materialism and Empirio-Criticism* was published. In this book he, as it were, "crossed all the t's and dotted all the i's" of this controversy. In Lenin's opinion the questions of philosophy were closely bound up with the question of the struggle against religion. That is why he delivered a lecture on *Religion and the Working Class* at the *Proletarii* Club and wrote an article entitled "The Attitude of the Workers' Party Towards Religion" for No. 45 of the *Proletarii* and another article entitled "The Attitude of Classes and Parties Towards Religion" for No. 6 of the *Sotsial Demokrat*.† These articles, particularly the one in *Proletarii*, are applicable to this very day. In these articles Ilyich emphasises the class character of religion and points out that in the hands of the bourgeoisie religion is a means for diverting the masses from the class struggle and for stultifying their minds. The fight on this front, he argues, must not be ignored or underestimated; but it must not be approached from too

---

* To which all the contributors and others actually connected with the paper were to be invited in addition to the board.—Ed.

† See *Lenin on Religion*. Little Lenin Library, Vol. VII.

simple an angle; the social roots of religion must be revealed, the question must be taken in all its complexity.

Even as a boy of fifteen, Ilyich understood the pernicious character of religion. He then ceased to wear a cross and stopped going to church. In those days this was not so simple a matter as it is now.

Lenin was of the opinion that the more subtle religions, those that were free from obvious absurdities and of external slavish forms were more pernicious than the rest. Such religions, he thought, were likely to exercise greater influence on people. He regarded god-creating,* attempts to create new religions and new beliefs as such a subtle religion.

In June the delegates began to assemble for the enlarged meeting of the editorial board of *Proletarii*. This enlarged editorial board of *Proletarii* was, in fact, the Bolshevik centre, which at that time also included the adherents of *Vperyod* (*Forward*).

Golubkov (Davidov), a Party worker who worked in the Bureau of the Central Committee in Russia under the direction of Innokenty and who was present at the Paris Conference in 1908, arrived from Moscow. Shulyatikov (Donat) and Shurkanov, a member of the Duma (who later proved to be an *agent provocateur*) also arrived. But he did not come to attend the conference. According to French custom our comrades took him to the café where he and Shulyatikov spent their time drinking beer. But Shulyatikov could not stand the drink; he suffered from hereditary alcoholism. The beer he drank caused a severe nervous fit, and on leaving the café he suddenly attacked Shurkanov with his walking stick. Innokenty and Golubkov barely managed to

* "God creators," also "God seekers," the name given to Bogdanov and his followers, Lunacharsky and others.—Ed.

D

restrain him. They brought him to our house. I
remained at home with him while they went to look
for a doctor, and a room for him somewhere in the
suburbs. They found a room on the Fontenay-aux-
Roses, where Semashko and Vladimirsky lived.

For two hours I stayed with the sick Shulyatikov
in our bare living room. He tossed about nervously,
jumped up, and had visions all the time of his sister
who had been hanged. I tried to calm him and to
distract his thoughts. I held his hand and this
seemed to have a soothing effect. No sooner would
I take my hand away than he became restless again.
I waited impatiently for Innokenty and Golubkov to
come for him.

Among those who attended the enlarged meeting
of the editorial board of *Proletarii* were Lenin,
Zinoviev, Kamenev, Bogdanov, representatives of the
Bolshevik organisations in Russia—Tomsky (St.
Petersburg), Shulyatikov (Moscow), Nakoryakov
(Urals); members of the Central Committee—Inno-
kenty, Rykov, Goldenberg, Taratuta and Marat
(Shantser). Besides these there were also present
Skrypnik (Shchur), Liubimov (Mark Zommer),
Poletaev (a member of the Third Duma) and
Davidov-Golubkov. The meeting lasted from July
4th to 13th.

Resolutions were passed on the Otzovists and
Ultimatists for Party unity and against the holding
of a special Bolshevik Congress. A special question
discussed at the meeting was that of the Capri
school. Bogdanov realised that the Bolshevik
fraction would inevitably break up and he, in antici-
pation of this, was beginning to select and organise his
own fraction. In Capri, Bogdanov, Alexinsky, Gorki
and Lunacharsky had organised a Social-Democratic
propagandist school for workers. A worker named

Vilonov recruited students for the school in Russia, and his instructions were to recruit "strong and reliable" men. After the experiences of the revolution, the workers strongly felt the need for theoretical training; moreover, this was a time when the immediate struggle had died down and there was time for this sort of thing. The workers went to Capri to study, but to everyone who had been in the thick of Party work it was clear that the Capri school would lay the foundations for a new fraction. And so, the enlarged meeting of the editorial board of *Proletarii* passed a resolution condemning the organisation of this new fraction. Bogdanov declared that he would not submit to the decision of the meeting and was expelled from the fraction. Krassin came out in his defence. The Bolshevik fraction split.

In the spring, even before the meeting of the editorial board of *Proletarii*, Maria Ilyinishna fell seriously ill. Ilyich was very much alarmed. Fortunately the disease was checked in time by an operation performed by Dubouchier. Her convalescence, however, was rather slow. She needed a rest outside of Paris in the country.

The conference put a great strain upon Ilyich, and when it was over it was necessary for him to go to the country for a rest, away from the turmoil and squabbling of emigré life.

Ilyich began to scan the French newspapers for advertisements of cheap boarding-houses. He found a boarding house in the village of Bon-Bon in the region of the Seine and Loire which only charged ten francs per day for four persons. We found the place very convenient and lived there about a month.

Ilyich did no work at Bon-Bon and we tried to refrain from discussing Party affairs. We went for walks every day and almost every day cycled to the

Clamar forests, fifteen kilometres away. We also observed French ways of life. Most of the guests at our boarding-house were office employees, shop assistants, etc. One was a saleswoman at a fashionable store, who was staying with her husband and daughter. Another was a valet to some Count. It was quite interesting to watch this petty-bourgeois crowd with its strongly marked petty-bourgeois mentality. On the one hand, these people were highly practical, and saw to it that they were well fed, and that everything was made comfortable for them. On the other hand, they all aspired to be regarded as real gentry. Madame Lagourette (this was the name of the saleswoman) was typical of the rest. She was obviously a woman of the world. She had a great fund of suggestive stories which she would relate with great gusto. But that did not prevent her from speaking longingly of the time when she would lead her daughter Marthe to her first communion, how touching that would be, etc., etc. Of course, to a large degree, this mediocrity bored us. It was a good thing that we were able to keep aloof from them and live as we wanted to. On the whole, Ilyich had a good rest at Bon-Bon.

In the autumn we changed our quarters. We moved to an apartment in the same neighbourhood in Rue Marie Rose. We had two rooms and a kitchen —our windows looked out on a garden. Our "living room" was now the kitchen, where all the heart-to-heart talks took place. By spring Vladimir was eager to set to work. He established a certain routine, as he called it. He would get up at eight o'clock in the morning, go to the Bibliothèque Nationale, return at 2 p.m. He also did a lot of work at home. I tried to keep people away from him. We always had many visitors, crowds upon crowds, especially at this time when, owing to the reaction raging in Russia, and the trying conditions of work, emigration from Russia increased very considerably. People would arrive from Russia and relate with enthusiasm what was going on there, but soon they seemed to wilt. They became submerged in the daily effort to earn a living and the petty worries of life.

At this time the students at the Capri school invited Ilyich to come to Capri to lecture there. Ilyich categorically refused. He explained to them the fractional character of the school and asked them to come to Paris. Within the Capri school, a fractional struggle flared up. In the beginning of November, five students (there were twelve in all) including Vilonov, the organiser of the school, officially declared themselves to be staunch Leninists and were expelled from the school. This incident proved better than anything else how right Lenin was when he pointed to the fractional character of the school. The expelled students came to Paris. I remember the first meeting we had with Vilonov. He began to tell us about his work in Ekaterinoslav. We had frequently received letters from a worker correspondent in Ekaterinoslav, who signed himself "Misha Zavodski." His letters were very interesting and dealt with the most vital questions of Party and factory life. "Do you happen to know Misha Zavodski?" I asked Vilonov. "Why, I am he," he answered. This immediately created a friendly feeling in Ilyich towards Michael and they had a very long talk that day. In the evening of that same day Ilyich wrote to Gorki as follows: "Dear Alexey Maximich: All this time I have been fully convinced that you and Comrade Michael were the staunchest champions of the new fraction, and with whom it would be absurd for me to attempt to speak in a friendly way. To-day

I met Comrade Michael for the first time. We had a
heart-to-heart talk about affairs and about yourself
and I realised that I had been greatly mistaken. By
gad! Philosopher Hegel was right: life progresses in
contradictions, and living contradictions are much
richer, more varied and profound than the human
mind can at first grasp. I regarded the school merely
as a centre of a new fraction. This proved to be
wrong—not in the sense that it is not the centre of a
new fraction (the school has been and is such a
centre) but in the sense that this is not complete, it is
not the whole truth. Subjectively, certain persons
were making the school such a centre; objectively,
it was such a centre; but in addition to this, it drew
from real working-class life real advanced workers."
And what an ardent confidence is expressed in the
strength of the working class at the end of the letter
where Lenin writes that the working class must
forge a party out of elements of every kind and every
calibre. "No matter what happens," he writes, "an
excellent, revolutionary, social-democracy will be
forged in Russia much sooner than it seems to us
looking at it from the angle of this thrice cursed state
of exile; it will be forged much more surely than we
imagine, if we are to judge by certain external symptoms and certain incidents. Men like Michael are a
guarantee of this."

Five other students of the Capri school arrived
with Michael. Among them "Vanya Kazanets"
(Pankratov) was the most conspicuous for his
activity and straightforwardness. His opposition to
the Capri school was more sharply expressed than
that of the rest. There was also Lushvin (Pakhon),
Kozyrev (Foma), Ustinov (Vasily) and Romanov
(Alya Alexinsky). Ilyich delivered a series of lectures
to them and devoted a great deal of attention to their

studies. Then they left for Russia, except Michael who had tuberculosis, which he had contracted as a result of the harsh treatment he had received in the Nikolayev penal regiment. We placed him in Davos. He did not live there long, however. He died on May 1st, 1910.

At the end of December the studies at Capri came to a close and the rest of the students arrived in Paris. Ilyich delivered lectures to these also. He spoke to them on current topics, about the land reforms introduced in Russia by the then premier Stolypin whose policy was to build up a class of "well-to-do" peasants, about the leading rôle of the proletariat and about the work of the Social-Democratic deputies in the Duma. Comrade Kozyrev relates that one of the students tried to trip Ilyich up and make it appear that Ilyich attached more importance to work in the Duma than to carrying on agitation in the army. Ilyich smiled, and went on to talk about the importance of work in the Duma. Of course, he did not for a moment think that the work in the army should be slackened in the least degree, but he did think that this work ought to be carried on more secretly. "This work," he said, "must be done, but not talked about." Just at this time a letter had arrived from Toulon, from a group of sailors, Social-Democrats, on the cruiser *Slava* asking for literature and particularly for a person to be sent to carry on revolutionary work among the sailors. Ilyich sent a comrade there who had much experience in secret work and this comrade settled in Toulon. Of course, Ilyich did not even as much as hint about this to the students.

Although Lenin's thoughts were almost entirely taken up with Russia, he nevertheless made a careful study of the French labour movement. At that time the Socialist Party of France was opportunistic to the core. For example: In the spring of 1909 a great strike of postal employees broke out. The whole city was in a state of excitement over the event; but the Party kept aloof. "It is the business of the trade unions and not ours," the Party leaders said. To us Russians this division of labour, the Party's aloofness from an economic struggle, seemed positively monstrous.

Ilyich paid particular attention to the election campaign. The campaign did not seem to concern immediate political problems; it was all taken up with personal bickering and mutual abuse. Only a few of the meetings were interesting. At one of them I saw Jaurès. He had tremendous influence on the crowd; but I did not like his speech—every word seemed to be deliberately chosen. I liked Vaillant's speech much better. Vaillant had been a fighter in the Paris Commune and was particularly loved and esteemed by the workers. I can recall the figure of a tall worker who had come to the meeting straight from work, with his shirt sleeves rolled up. This man listened to Vaillant with wrapt attention and suddenly he exclaimed: "Fine speaker, the old man!" Two young lads, the sons of this worker, sitting beside him, were equally enthusiastic. But not all the orators at the meetings were Jaurèses and Vaillants. The ordinary speakers played down to their audiences: they spoke in one way to a working-class audience and in another way to an audience of intellectuals. By attending French election meetings, we got a clear insight into what elections mean in a "democratic republic." To an outside observer, the thing seemed simply astonishing. That is why Ilyich was so fond of the revolutionary music-hall singers who poured ridicule on the election campaign. I remember one song which described how a candidate goes to a village to canvass for votes; he drinks with the peasants, tells them a lot of cock-and-bull stories, and when the peasants are drunk they vote for him and sing "T'as ben dit mon ga!" (What you say is true, lad!). After having got the peasants' votes, the candidate begins to draw his 15,000 francs salary as deputy, and betrays the interests of the peasants. On one occasion a Socialist member of the Chamber of Deputies named Dumas came to visit us and related to us how he went around the villages during the election to canvass for votes and I involuntarily called to mind that music-hall song. One of the most popular music-hall singers of that time was Montagus, the son of a fighter in the Paris Commune; he was the favourite of the faubourgs (the working-class districts). His songs combined the sentimentality of the petty bourgeois with the spirit of the true revolutionary.

Ilyich was fond of visiting the suburban theatres, and of watching the working-class audiences there. I remember on one occasion we went to see a play which depicted the tortures of soldiers in a penal battalion in Morocco. It was most interesting to watch the audience. They were quick to respond to every incident. The performance had not yet begun. Suddenly shouts went up from all over the theatre: "Hat! Hat!" This outburst was caused by the entry of a lady wearing a fashionable hat trimmed with feathers. The audience demanded that the lady remove her hat and she was obliged to submit. The performance began. In the play a soldier is sent to Morocco and his mother and sister remain at home in poverty. The landlord of the house in which they live is willing to allow them to live there without paying the rent if the soldier's sister agrees to become his mistress. "Brute! Dirty dog!" was shouted from all parts of the hall. I have forgotten all the details of the play, but I remember that it depicts how the soldiers who do not submit to the officers are tortured in Morocco. It ended with a mutiny and the singing of the *Internationale*. The performance of this play was prohibited in the centre of the city; but in the suburbs it was performed to enthusiastic audiences. In 1910 a huge demonstration took place in which about 100,000 persons took part, to protest against the Morocco adventure. The demonstration took place with the sanction of the police. It was headed by Socialist members of the Chamber of Deputies who wore red sashes. The workers were in a fighting mood and shook their fists at the windows of the houses in the wealthy quarters of the town. Here and there shutters were hastily put up; but the demonstration passed off as peacefully as could be. It did not resemble a protest demonstration at all.

Through Charles Rappoport, Vladimir Ilyich was introduced to Paul Lafargue, a son-in-law of Karl Marx, a true and tried fighter of whom Ilyich had a very high opinion. Lafargue and his wife Laura, Marx's daughter, lived in Dravelle, about 25 kilometres from Paris. They had already retired from active work. One day, Ilyich and I cycled to Dravelle to visit the Lafargues. They received us very amiably. Vladimir began to tell Lafargue about his book on philosophy while Laura Lafargue took me for a walk in the park. I was a little excited —I was actually walking with Marx's daughter. I scanned her face eagerly to try to find some resemblance to Marx in her features. In my embarrassment I babbled something inarticulately about the part women were playing in the revolutionary

movement and about Russia. She replied, but somehow or other conversation lagged. When we returned
we found Lafargue and Ilyich discussing philosophy.
"Soon he will prove," Laura said about her husband,
"how sincere are his philosophic convictions," and
she exchanged significant glances with her husband.
In 1911, when I learned of the death of the Lafargues,
I understood the significance of these words and
of this exchange of glances. They both died together
as atheists. They committed suicide and left a note
saying that they had both decided to die because
of their old age, and because they were too feeble to
carry on the struggle.

   In 1910 an enlarged meeting of the Central Committee of the Party was held. At the enlarged meeting of the editorial board of the *Proletarii*, resolutions
had been passed in favour of Party unity and against
calling a separate Bolshevik Congress. At this meeting of the Central Committee Ilyich and a group of
comrades who rallied round him maintained the
same line. In the period of reaction it was extremely
important to have a party that boldly told the whole
truth, even though it was underground. This was a
time when the reaction was wrecking the Party,
when the Party was becoming submerged in opportunism, when it was important to hold aloft the
banner of the Party at all cost. In Russia, the
liquidators had their own strong, legal opportunist
centre. It was necessary to retain the Party in order
to counteract that centre. The experience of the
Capri school showed how very often at that time the
fractionalism of the workers was relative and peculiar.
It was important to have a united Party centre
around which the masses of the Social-Democratic
workers could rally. The struggle in 1910 was a
struggle for the very existence of the Party, for exer-

cising influence upon the workers through the medium of the Party. Vladimir Ilyich was convinced that within the Party the Bolsheviks would be in the majority, that in the end the Party would take the Bolshevik line; but it had to be a Party and not a fraction. Ilyich pursued this line also in 1911 when a Party school was being formed near Paris which admitted the followers of *Vperyod* and Party Mensheviks* as well as Bolsheviks. This line was also pursued at the Prague Party Conference in 1912. Ilyich did not want a fraction but a Party that pursued a Bolshevik line. Of course, in this Party there was no room for liquidators, for the fight against whom forces were being gathered. Of course, there was no room in the Party for those who had decided beforehand that they would not abide by the decisions of the Party. Certain comrades, however, interpreted the fight for the Party to mean conciliation with the liquidators; they lost sight of the purpose of unity and strove to unite everybody irrespective of what their aims were. Even Innokenty, who entirely supported Lenin's point of view, and who considered that the main thing was to unite with the Party Mensheviks, with the Plekhanovists, was so carried away with the desire to preserve the Party that he, too, began to incline towards the conciliatory point of view. Ilyich put him right, however.

On the whole, the resolutions were passed unanimously. It is ridiculous to think that Ilyich was voted down and overwhelmed by the votes of the conciliators and that he surrendered his position. The Plenum lasted three weeks. Ilyich considered that it was necessary to make the utmost possible concessions on organisational questions without yielding an inch

---

* I.e. Mensheviks who were not liquidators; who agreed that the illegal Party should be preserved.—Ed.

of his position on principles. *Proletarii*, the organ of
the Bolshevik fraction, was closed down. The 500-
ruble notes which had not yet been changed were
destroyed. The funds of the Bolshevik fraction were
handed over to so-called "trustees," three German
comrades: Kautsky, Mehring, and Clara Zetkin,
who were to pay out the money only for general
Party purposes; in the event of a split the balance of
the money was to be returned to the Bolsheviks.
Kamenev was sent to Vienna as the Bolshevik representative on the Trotskyist *Pravda*. "Things have
been very stormy here recently," Lenin wrote to his
sister, Anna Ilyinishna, "but it ended in an attempt to
make peace with the Mensheviks. Yes, yes, strange as
it may appear, we have closed down the organ of the
fraction and we are trying to make a strong move
towards unity."

Innokenty and Nogin went to Russia to organise a
Russian (i.e. working in Russia) collegium of the
Central Committee. Nogin was a conciliator who
wished to unite everybody and his speeches met with
a rebuff on the part of the Bolsheviks. Innokenty
followed a different line; but Russia was not
"abroad" where every word uttered was understood:
his words were interpreted in the terms of Nogin, all
the non-Bolsheviks saw to that. Lindov and V. P.
Miliutin were co-opted on the Central Committee.
Innokenty was soon arrested. Lindov shared Nogin's
point of view, and was not very active. The state of
the Russian Central Committee in 1910 could not
have been worse.

Abroad, things were not much better. Mark
(Liubimov) and Lyova (Vladimirov) were "conciliators in general" and frequently allowed themselves
to be influenced by tales about the alleged quarrelsomeness and disloyalty of the Bolsheviks. Mark,

particularly, heard many such stories, for he was a member of the United Bureau of the Central Committee Abroad, on which all the fractions were represented.

The *Vperyod*-ists continued to organise their forces. Alexinsky's group once broke into a meeting of a Bolshevik group which had assembled in a café on Avenue d'Orléans. With an insolent air Alexinsky sat down at a table and demanded to be allowed to speak, and when this was refused he began to create an uproar. The *Vperyod*-ists who came with him threw themselves upon our comrades to attack them. Abram Skovno and Isaac Krivoy, members of our group, were about to plunge into the fight, but Nikolai Vassilievich Sapozhkov (Kuznetsov), a very powerful man, grabbed him under one arm and Isaac under the other, while the proprietor of the café, who had had much experience in the matter of brawls, extinguished the lights. There was no fight. But after this incident Ilyich wandered about the streets of Paris all night and when he returned home he could not fall asleep until morning.

In a letter to Maxim Gorki dated April 11th, 1910, Ilyich wrote: "Well, it seems that the 'ludicrous' is the predominant note in the unity and gives good grounds for sniggering, jokes, etc. It is sickening to have to live amidst this 'ludicrousness,' amidst this squabbling and scandal. And it is sickening to watch it. But one must not give way to one's moods. The life of an exile now is a hundred times more arduous than it was before the revolution. Exile and squabbling are inseparable. But squabbling is a minor thing; nine-tenths of the squabbling remains abroad; squabbling is merely a by-product. But the development of the Party, the development of the Social-Democratic movement is going on and on, in spite of the present hellishly difficult conditions. The purging of the Social-Democratic Party of its dangerous 'deviations,' of its liquidationism and Otzovism is going ahead unswervingly; within the framework of unity it has made considerably more progress than before."

Further on, he writes: "I can imagine how hard it is to watch this difficult growth of a new Social-Democratic movement for those who have not seen and did not experience the difficult growth at the end of the eighties and the beginning of the nineties. At that time Social-Democrats could be counted in tens if not in units. Now they number hundreds and thousands. Hence, crisis after crisis. And Social-Democracy *as a whole* is overcoming these crises openly and honestly."

Sick of the squabbling, a number of the comrades went away. Lozovsky,* for example, gave himself up entirely to the French trade union movement. We, too, longed to come closer to the French movement. We thought it would be useful for us in this connection if we went to live for a time at the holiday camp organised by the French Party. This camp was situated on the sea shore near the village of Pornic on the famous Vendée coast. First my mother and I went to live there, but we were not happy there. The French people kept too much to themselves; each family kept aloof from the others and their attitude towards Russians was somewhat unfriendly. This was particularly the case with the manager of the camp. I became rather friendly with a French teacher. There were hardly any workers at the camp. Soon, the Kostitsins and Savvushka, *Vperyod*-ists, arrived at the camp, and they immediately had a row with the manager. Then we all decided to move to Pornic and board together. My mother and

* Now head of the Red International of Labour Unions.—Ed.

I rented two small rooms from the coast-guard. Soon Ilyich arrived. He bathed in the sea a great deal, cycled—he loved the sea and the sea breezes—and chatted cheerfully on all sorts of subjects with the Kostitsins, enjoyed eating the crabs which the coast-guard caught for us. In fact, our landlord and his wife took a great liking to Ilyich. The stout, loud-voiced landlady—she was a laundress—would tell us about the conflicts she had with the priests. She had a little son who attended the secular school, and since the youngster was a clever and capable boy, the priests tried to persuade the mother to allow the boy to be educated in the monastery and promised to pay the boy a scholarship; but the laundress indignantly showed the priest the door. She did not give birth to a son, she said, in order to make a despicable Jesuit of him. And this was why Ilyich praised the crabs so highly. Ilyich arrived at Pornic on August 1st, and by the 26th he was already in Copenhagen whither he had gone to attend the meeting of the International Socialist Bureau and the International Socialist Congress. In describing the work of the Congress, Ilyich wrote: "Differences with the revisionists are looming, but the revisionists are still far from a declaration of their own independent programme. The struggle against revisionism has been postponed, but this struggle is inevitable." The Russian delegation at the Congress was a large one—twenty in all: ten Social-Democrats, seven Socialist-Revolutionaries and three trade-union delegates. The Social-democratic group contained representatives of every shade: Lenin, Zinoviev, Kamenev, Plekhanov, Varsky, Martov and Martinov. Trotsky, Lunacharsky and Kollontai were also in the delegation with consultative votes.* During the

* I.e. the right to speak but not to vote.—Ed.

Congress a conference took place in which Lenin, Plekhanov, Zinoviev and the members of the Third Duma, Poletaev and I. P. Pokrovsky, took part. At this conference it was decided to publish a popular newspaper abroad to be called *Rabochaya Gazeta* (*Workers' Newspaper*). Plekhanov played a diplomatic game; nevertheless, he wrote an article for the first number of the paper entitled "Our Position."

After the Copenhagen Congress, Ilyich went to Stockholm to see his mother and sister Maria Ilyinishna and spent ten days there. This was the last time he saw his mother. He had a premonition of that and it was with sad and wistful eyes that he followed the departing steamer. When he returned to Russia seven years later, in 1917, she was already dead.

On his return to Paris, Ilyich related that he had managed to have a good talk with Lunacharsky at the Congress. Ilyich always had a strong liking for Lunacharsky. He was greatly charmed by the latter's talent. However, soon after, an article by Lunacharsky entitled "Tactical Trends in Our Party" appeared in *Le Peuple*, in which he treated all the questions from the Otzovist point of view. Ilyich read the article and said nothing. But later, he wrote an article in reply. Others who attended the International Congress also wrote their opinion on it. Trotsky wrote an unsigned article in *Vorwärts*, in which he severely attacked the Bolsheviks and praised his own Vienna *Pravda*. Plekhanov, Lenin and Varsky sent a protest to *Vorwärts* for publishing this article. As far back as 1903 when Trotsky made his appearance abroad, Plekhanov was already hostile towards him. Before the Second Party Congress they had a serious dispute on the question of publishing a popular newspaper. At the Copenhagen Congress Plekhanov signed a protest against Trotsky's action

E

without a word. In retaliation, Trotsky started a campaign against the *Rabochaya Gazeta*, which the Bolsheviks were beginning to publish. He declared that *Rabochaya Gazeta* was a narrow fraction organ, and he also delivered a lecture on this subject at the Vienna Club. As a protest against this, Kamenev resigned from the editorial board of the Trotskyist *Pravda* to which he had been appointed after the January Plenum. The Paris conciliators led by Mark were influenced by Trotsky's campaign, and they, too, began a campaign against *Rabochaya Gazeta*, on the grounds that they were fighting factionalism. Ilyich hated this vague conciliationism that was devoid of all principle, conciliation with anybody and everybody, which in his opinion was tantamount to surrendering the position when the battle was at its height.

Neue Zeit, No. 50 of 1910, contained an article by Trotsky entitled "Tendencies in the Development of Russian Social-Democracy," and No. 51 contained an article by Martov on "Russian Discussion and Russian Experience." Vladimir Ilyich replied to these in an article entitled "The Historic Significance of the Internal Struggle of the Party in Russia," but the editors of *Neue Zeit*, Kautsky and Wurm, refused to publish it. Markhlevsky (Karsky) replied to Trotsky and Martov by letter after consulting Vladimir Ilyich.

In 1911 Comrade Kamo arrived in Paris. He was the comrade who was arrested in Berlin in 1908 while carrying a valise filled with dynamite. He was kept in a German prison for over eighteen months, and while there he pretended to be insane. In October 1909 he was deported to Russia, and there spent another sixteen months in the Metekh fortress in Tiflis. The prison doctor came to the conclusion

that Kamo was hopelessly insane and had him transferred to the Mikhailovsk mental hospital. He escaped from the hospital, stowed away on a ship
bound for France, and finally arrived in Paris to
talk things over with Ilyich. He was terribly upset
when he heard that a rupture had occurred between
Ilyich and Bogdanov and Krassin. He was very
much attached to all three, besides, he did not
understand the situation that had developed during
the years he was in prison. Ilyich told him all that
had occurred.

Kamo asked me to buy him almonds. He would
sit in our kitchen living-room eating almonds as he
had done at home and would tell us about his arrest
in Berlin, about the way he had simulated insanity,
about the sparrow he tamed in prison, etc. Ilyich
would listen and feel extremely sorry for this exceedingly brave, childishly naïve, warm-hearted
man who was capable of performing heroic feats, but
who now did not know what work to take up. The
proposals he made were fantastic. Ilyich did not
contradict him, but carefully brought him back to
earth, talked to him about the necessity of organising
the transport of literature, etc. Finally it was decided
that Kamo should go to Belgium to have an operation performed on his eyes (he was cross-eyed, and
this enabled spies to identify him very easily), and
then make his way to the south of Russia and from
there to the Caucasus. Examining Kamo's coat,
Ilyich asked: "Have you got a warm coat? You will
be cold on deck in this one." Whenever Ilyich
travelled on a steamer he walked up and down the
deck incessantly. When it turned out that Kamo had
no other coat, Ilyich took his soft grey cloak which
his mother had given him as a present while in Stockholm, and of which he was very fond, and gave it to

Kamo. The talk with Ilyich and Ilyich's kindness soothed Kamo. Years after, during the civil war, Kamo again found his "element" and again performed miracles of heroism. It is true that when we adopted the new economic policy he again went off the rails and kept talking about wanting to go to school, dreaming all the while of all kinds of exploits. He died at the time of Ilyich's last illness. He was cycling down the Veryesk slope in Tiflis, ran into an automobile and was killed.

In 1910 Inessa Armand arrived from Brussels and immediately became an active member of our Paris group. Together with Semashko and Brittman (Kazakov) she joined the committee of the group and began to carry on extensive correspondence with other groups abroad. She had two little children, a boy and girl. She was a very ardent Bolshevik and soon gathered our Paris crowd around her.

On the whole, our Paris group began to grow and gained strength. Ideologically, we also became stronger. The only trouble was that we were so poor. Workers managed to eke out a livelihood somehow or other, but the conditions of the intellectuals were very bad. It was not always possible to become a worker. To live at the expense of the exiles' funds and to feed in the exiles' dining-room was humiliating. I remember several sad cases. One comrade tried to become a French polisher, but it was not easy to learn the trade, and he was forced to change his jobs frequently. He lived in a working-class district far from where the other exiles lived. At last he became so weak from lack of food that he could not leave his bed and wrote to us asking for money. He asked, however, that it should not be brought directly to him but left with the concierge.

Nikolai Vasilievich Sapozhkov (Kuznetsov) had a hard time. He and his wife found work at painting pottery, but they earned very little and one could see this giant of a man positively withering away; his face became furrowed with wrinkles as a result of slow starvation, although he never complained of his condition. There were many cases like that. The saddest case of all was that of Comrade Prigara, who had taken part in the Moscow uprising. He lived somewhere in a working-class suburb, and the comrades knew little about him. One day he came to us and began to talk excitedly and incoherently about chariots filled with sheaves of corn and about beautiful girls standing on the chariots, etc., etc. It was obvious that the man was insane. Our first thought was that it was due to starvation. Mother began to prepare something to eat for him. Ilyich, his face pale with pity, remained with Prigara while I ran to call a friend of ours who was a mental specialist. The latter came, had a talk with the sick man, and said that it was a serious case of insanity, brought on by starvation. The case was not critical, he said, but it would devlop into a persecution mania and the patient was likely to commit suicide. He had to be watched. We did not even know his address. Brittman went to see him home, but on the way he disappeared. We roused our group and organised a search, but in vain. Later, his corpse was found in the Seine with stones tied to his neck and feet—he had committed suicide.

To have lived another year or two in this atmosphere would have been fatal. But the years of reaction gave way to years of revival of the revolutionary movement.

In connection with the death of Tolstoi, demonstrations were organised in Russia. The first

issue of *Zvezda* (*The Star*) was published, in Moscow
the Bolshevik *Mysl* (*Thought*) began to appear.
Ilyich immediately revived. His article: "The
Beginning of the Demonstrations," written on
December 31st, 1910, breathes inexhaustible energy.
It ends up with the invocation: "To work, comrades! Begin everywhere to build up your organisations, to create and strengthen Social-Democratic
workers' cells, to develop economic and political
agitation. In the first Russian revolution the proletariat taught the masses of the people to fight for
liberty; in the second revolution it must lead them
to victory."

THE YEARS OF THE REVOLUTIONARY REVIVAL
(1911-14)

PARIS
(1911-12)

THE end of 1910 was marked by the revolutionary revival. The years from 1911 to 1914 were years in which, right up to the beginning of the war in August 1914, every month saw an increase in the strength of the labour movement. But this movement was now growing under conditions entirely different from those in which the labour movement grew before 1905. It was developing on the basis of the experiences of the 1905 revolution. It was not the same proletariat. The proletariat had gone through a great deal—a wave of strikes, a number of armed uprisings, a tremendous mass movement; and it had experienced years of defeat. That made all the difference. This was reflected in everything, and Ilyich, who flung himself with all his ardour into the maelstrom of life and was able to discern the significance of and weigh every phrase uttered by the workers, felt this growth of the proletariat in every fibre of his being. On the other hand, he knew that it was not only the proletariat but that conditions as a whole had changed. The intelligentsia, too, had changed. In 1905, broad strata of the intelligentsia supported the workers. Now it was different. The character of the struggle that was to be led by the proletariat had already become defined. The struggle would be fierce, irreconcilable; the proletariat would destroy everything that stood in its way. The liberal bourgeoisie would no longer be able to use the workers as a tool for the purpose of winning for itself the limited Constitution that it wanted. The working class would not be content with a limited Constitution. The working class would not be led; it would lead. And the conditions of the struggle changed, too. The tsarist government had also learned the lessons of the 1905 revolution. It had now enmeshed the entire labour organisation with a network of *agents provocateurs*. These were not the old type of spies who used to hang around street corners, and from whom it was possible to hide. These were the Malinovskys, Romanovs, the Brendinskys, the Chernomazovs, who had managed to penetrate into the Party and occupy responsible positions in it. The spying and arrests were no longer haphazard; they were carefully planned.

These conditions served as a regular breeding-ground for opportunism of the worst kind. The policy of the liquidators to dissolve the Party, the vanguard of the working class, was supported by the broad strata of the intelligentsia. Liquidators sprang up right and left like mushrooms. Every insignificant cadet* tried to throw mud at the illegal Party. It was impossible not to carry on a fierce struggle against them. The struggle, however, was an unequal one. The liquidators had a strong legal centre in Russia and were able to carry on extensive work in favour of their policy among the masses. The Bolsheviks, on the other hand, had to fight for every inch of the ground, under the very trying con-

* Abbreviation of the term Constitutional Democrat, i.e. bourgeois liberal.—Ed.

ditions of underground work which then prevailed.

The year 1911 started with a break-through of the censorship on the one hand and an energetic struggle for the strengthening of the illegal Party organisation on the other. The fight began inside the united organisation abroad, which was created at the conference of January 1910; but soon it extended beyond the limits of this organisation and pursued its own course. Ilyich was overjoyed at the publication of *Zvezda* in St. Petersburg and *Mysl* in Moscow. The organisation of the shipment to Russia of the newspapers published abroad was very bad indeed, worse than it was before 1905. Russia and the foreign countries were teeming with *agents provocateurs*, who managed to get on the track of everything. Hence Ilyich's joy at the publication in Russia of legal newspapers and magazines to which Bolsheviks could contribute.

The editorial board of *Zvezda* consisted of Bonch-Bruevich (Bolshevik), N. Jordansky (a follower of Plekhanov at that time) and I. Pokrovsky (a member of the Duma who sympathised with the Bolsheviks). The newspaper was the organ of the Social-Democratic Party in the Duma.* The first issue contained an article by Plekhanov. Vladimir Ilyich was not quite satisfied with the first issue, it appeared dull to him. But he was very pleased with the first issue of the Moscow *Mysl*.

Writing to Maxim Gorki about the paper, he said: "It is *entirely* ours and it pleases me greatly." Ilyich began to write a great deal for *Zvezda* and *Mysl*. It was not an easy task to publish legal newspapers at that time. In February Skvortsov-Stepanov was arrested in Moscow, and in St. Petersburg Bonch-Bruevich, Lydia Mikhailovna Knipovich who

* Referred to as the Duma fraction.—Ed.

worked with Poletaev and others were arrested. In April *Mysl* was completely closed down and in June, *Zvezda*, the organ of the Duma fraction was also discontinued after twenty-five numbers had been published. It did not resume publication until November 5th. It then became a definitely Bolshevik paper. In Baku another Bolshevik paper *Sovremyenaya Zhizn* (*Contemporary Life*) also began to be published.

In July negotiations with Comrade Savelyev commenced for the publication of a legal magazine *Prosveshchenie* (*Education*) in St. Petersburg, but we succeeded in publishing this magazine only at the end of 1911.

Vladimir Ilyich watched these publications very closely and wrote for them.

With regard to establishing connections with the workers—at first, attempts were made to educate the students of the Bologna school in the same way as was done with the students of the Capri school, but nothing came of this.

In November 1910, the Otzovists organised a school in Bologna, Italy. The students invited a number of lecturers to lecture to them. Among these were Dan, Plekhanov and Lenin. Vladimir Ilyich refused to go to Bologna but asked the students to come to Paris. The *Vperyod*-ists, having learned from the experience of the Capri school, began to hedge; they demanded an official invitation from the Bureau of the Central Committee abroad in which the Mensheviks predominated at that time. And when they arrived in Paris together with the students who were to counteract Lenin's influence, they demanded autonomy. However, no studies were organised and the bureau sent the students back to Russia.

In the spring of 1911 we at last succeeded in establishing our own Party school near Paris. This school was open to Bolshevik workers and Party Menshevik and *Vperyod*-ist (Otzovist) workers. The two latter groups, however, were a small minority.

The first to arrive at the school were comrades from St. Petersburg—two metal workers—Belostotsky (Vladimir) and George (I cannot recall his surname), a *Vperyod*-ist, and a woman worker named Vera Vasilyeva. They were an intelligent group and quite advanced. On the first evening of their arrival Ilyich took them to a café for supper and I remember how fervently he spoke to them the whole evening, asking them about St. Petersburg, about their work, and trying to detect in their answers symptoms of the revival of the labour movement in Russa. Nicolai Alexandrovich Semashko got them temporarily fixed up in Fontenay-aux-Roses, a suburb of Paris, not far from where he lived. While waiting until the other students arrived they spent their time reading; later, two comrades arrived from Moscow: Prisyagin, a tanner by trade, and a textile worker whose name I do not remember. The St. Petersburg comrades soon became fast friends with Prisyagin. He was a worker above the average level of intelligence and had edited the illegal journal of the leather workers in Russia. He wrote well, but he was very shy. His hands would tremble with nervousness when he talked. Belostotsky teased him for this, but very mildly and good naturedly.

During the October revolution, Prisyagin was chairman of the Provincial Council of Trade Unions in Barnaul, in Siberia. He was caught and shot by Kolchak when the latter captured the city.

But Belostotsky made fun of the Moscow textile worker in by no means a kindly manner. This textile worker had not had much education, but he was very cock-sure. He wrote poems and talked in a high-flown manner. Once I visited the students at their rooms and met one of the Moscow comrades. He volunteered to call the other students together, and in doing so, he called out "Mister Krupskaya has come." For this "Mister Krupskaya" Belostotsky teased him unmercifully. There were constant conflicts between them. Finally, the St. Petersburgers began to insist that the fellow be removed from the school. " He does not understand anything and talks a lot of nonsense about prostitution," they said. We tried to convince them that the lad would learn better, but the St. Petersburgers insisted upon his being sent back to Moscow. We were obliged to remove him from the school and found temporary work for him in Germany.

We decided to organise the school in the village of Longjumeau, 15 kilometres from Paris, where there were no Russians and no summer visitors. Longjumeau was a straggling French village stretching along the highroad over which cartloads of farmers' produce rumbled all night carrying food to fill "the belly of Paris." There was a small tannery in the village situated in a field surrounded by orchards. Our plan was the following. The students were to rent rooms in the village. Inessa was to rent a whole house in which a dining-room was to be organised for the students. We and the Zinovievs also moved to Longjumeau. Katya Mazonova, the wife of a worker who had been in exile with Martov in Turukhansk in Siberia, and later had worked illegally in the Urals, undertook to keep house. Katya was a good housekeeper and a good comrade. Everything went off splendidly. In the house which Inessa

rented we placed Sergo (Ordjonikidze),* Simyon
(Schwartz) and Zakhar (Breslav). Sergo arrived in
Paris a little before that. Until then he had lived in
Persia and I remember the detailed correspondence
we carried on with him concerning the line which
Ilyich pursued in relation to the Plekhanovists, the
liquidators and the *Vperyod*-ists. We always maintained regular correspondence with the Caucasian
Bolshevik group. We had written to Sergo giving
the details of the struggle that was raging abroad and
for a long time we received no reply. One day the
concierge came in to me and said: "There's a man
downstairs who doesn't speak a word of French; he
must be looking for you." I went downstairs and saw
a smiling Caucasian standing in the hall. It proved
to be Sergo. From that time on he became one of our
most intimate comrades. Simyon Schwartz we had
known for a long time. My mother liked him particularly well, because he would relate in her pres-
ence how, when a lad of nineteen, he distributed
leaflets in a factory for the first time. He was a
worker from Nikolayev. While distributing the
leaflets, he pretended to be drunk, he said. Breslav
we had known since 1905 in St. Petersburg.

Thus, Inessa's house was entirely occupied by our
own people. We lived at the other end of the village,
and would take our dinner in the communal dining-
room, where it was pleasant to chat with the students, question them on various topics and discuss
current events with them.

We rented a couple of rooms in a small, two-story,
brick house (in Longjumeau all the houses were
built of brick), from a worker employed at the
tannery, and this gave us an opportunity to observe
the life of a worker employed in a small enterprise.

* Now Commissar for the Heavy Industries in the U.S.S.R.—Ed.

This man would go to work early in the morning and come back in the evening completely exhausted. There was no garden attached to this house. Sometimes, he would bring a table and a chair out into the street, and would sit for hours resting his tired head on his exhausted arms. None of his fellow workers ever visited him. On Sundays he would go to the church, the spire of which towered across the road. Music seemed to enrapture him. Nuns with beautiful opera voices would come to sing at the church; they would sing the compositions of Beethoven and others and it is not surprising that the tanner, whose life was so drab, should have been enraptured with the music. We could not help comparing him with Prisyagin who was also a tanner by trade and whose life was not much easier than that of the Longjumeau tanner; but he was a class-conscious fighter, and a favourite among his comrades. The wife of the French tanner would put on her wooden shoes early in the morning, take her broom and go to the neighbouring chateau where she was employed as a char-woman. Her young daughter would remain at home to look after the house. All day long she would stay in the gloomy, damp house, taking care of her younger brothers and sisters. She did not appear to have any girl friends. Her life was just one round of household drudgery on week-days and of visits to the church on Sundays and holidays. It never occurred to any of the members of the tanner's family that any change was required in the social system. Why, god created the rich and the poor, then things must be so—reasoned the tanner.

The French nursemaid whom the Zinovievs hired to take care of their three-year-old boy was also of this opinion, and when the youngster tried to make his way into the park of the chateau which adjoined Longjumeau, she would say to him: "This is not for us, this is for the gentry." We were greatly amused when the youngster, with an air of wisdom, repeated the words of his nurse.

Soon all the students were assembled, Andreyev, a worker from Nikolayev, who, while in exile, I think in Vologda, passed through a peculiar course of study. Ilyich would jestingly call him his best student. Then there was Dogadov from Baku (Pavel), and Sema (Semkov). Two arrived from Kiev; Andrey Malinovsky and Chugurin. These two were Plekhanovists. Later we discovered that Malinovsky was an *agent provocateur*. He was not distinguished in any way except that he had a beautiful voice. He was quite a young fellow and not very observant. He told me how he had eluded the police while on his way to Paris. His story did not seem very plausible to me, but it did not arouse any particular suspicion. The other man, Chugurin, regarded himself as a Plekhanovist. He was a worker employed at the Sormova works and had served a long term of imprisonment. He was a very intelligent worker, but rather highly strung. He soon became a Bolshevik. Savva (Zevin) also a Plekhanovist, came from Ekaterinoslav. When renting rooms for the students we said that they were Russian village teachers. During his stay at Longjumeau, Savva fell sick with typhus. The French doctor who visited him said smilingly; "What strange teachers you have." The thing that surprised the French people most was that our "teachers" would walk around all day barefooted. (It was unbearably hot that summer.)

Six months later Zevin attended the Paris Party Conference. He fought in the ranks of the Bolsheviks for many years until his tragic death. He was one of the twenty-six Baku Commissars who were shot by the White Guards in 1918.

Vasily (S. Iskryanistov) came from Ivanovo-Voznesensk. He was a very good student, but behaved rather strangely. He would lock himself up in his room and avoid everybody. When he returned to Russia he flatly refused to undertake any commission. He was a very capable worker, however. For a number of years he occupied responsible positions. He was terribly poor. In the factories he was looked upon as an "unreliable" and therefore found it difficult to keep his job. For a very long time he, his wife and two children, maintained themselves on the very meagre earnings of his wife who was a textile worker. As we discovered later, Iskryanistov could no longer bear the strain and became an *agent provocateur*. He began to drink heavily. In Longjumeau he was an abstainer, but when he returned to Russia he broke down altogether and committed suicide. One evening he drove his wife and children out of the house, lit the stove, stopped up the chimney and in the morning he was found dead. For his "work" as a *provocateur* he received a miserable "reward" of about ten rubles. He was a *provocateur* for less than a year.

Olyeg (Prukhnyak) represented the Poles. In the middle of the term Mantsev arrived.

Studies went on very regularly. Ilyich delivered lectures on political economy (thirty lectures), on the agrarian question (ten lectures), and on the theory and practice of socialism (five lectures). Inessa worked as a tutor on political economy. Zinoviev and Kamenev lectured on the history of the Party and Semashko also delivered several lectures. There were several other lecturers, among whom were Riazanov, who lectured on the history of the labour movement in western Europe, Charles Rappoport who lectured on the French labour movement, Steklov and Finn-Yenotaevsky lectured on public law and finance, Lunacharsky on literature, and Stanislav Volsky on journalism.

The students worked very hard, but some evenings they would go out into the field where they would sing or lie near a haystack and talk about all sorts of things. Ilyich would sometimes accompany them.

Kamenev did not live in Longjumeau and would come there only to deliver his lectures. At that time he was writing his book *Two Parties*. He would often discuss this with Ilyich. They would lie on the grass in the meadow on the outskirts of the village and Ilyich would expound his ideas. Ilyich wrote a preface to this book.

I had to go to Paris frequently to see our people on business. This was necessary in order to save them coming to Longjumeau. The students were preparing to go back to work in Russia, and it was necessary to keep their stay near Paris as secret as possible. Ilyich was very pleased with the work of the school. In our spare time we usually went cycling. We would walk up the hill and then ride out for about fifteen kilometres to a place where there was an aerodrome. This was a secluded place and much less frequented than the aerodrome at Juvissy. Often we were the only visitors and Ilyich was able to watch the manœuvres of the aeroplanes to his heart's content.

In the middle of August we moved back to Paris.

The unity of all the fractions, which was achieved with so much difficulty in 1910, gradually began to break up. As the practical problems of the work in Russia arose it became more and more clear that joint work was impossible. The requirements of

F

practical work tore away the mask that some of the
Mensheviks wore. The real meaning of Trotsky's
"loyalty" was revealed. Behind the mask of loyalty
he tried to unite the liquidators and the *Vperyod*-ists.
When it became necessary to improve the work of
the organisations in Russia the artificiality of this
unity immediately became revealed. At the end of
December 1910, Lenin, Zinoviev and Kamenev
had submitted a proposal to the Bureau of the Central
Committee abroad urging the necessity of convening
a Plenum of the Central Committee. More than a
month passed before they received a reply. The
Menshevik Bureau of the Central Committee abroad
rejected the proposal. Negotiations on this subject
dragged on until the end of May 1911. It became
obvious that no good would come out of the Bureau.
Comrade Semashko, who was the Bolshevik representative on the Bureau, resigned and the Bolsheviks
convened a Conference of the members of the
Central Committee who were abroad at that time.
In June 1911 there were nine members of the
Central Committee abroad. All except the Bundist,
Iyonov, who was sick, assembled on June 10th, but
the Menshevik Goriev and the Bundist leader left
the conference. Those who remained discussed the
most pressing questions confronting the Party and
also the question of convening a Party Conference.
It was decided to set up an organisation committee
in Russia, the function of which was to make
arrangements for the Party Conference. In August
the comrades left for Russia. Breslav (Zakhar) went
to St. Petersburg and Moscow, Simyon (Schwartz)
went to the Urals and to Ekaterinoslav, and Sergo
went to the south. Rykov also went to Russia, but
was arrested in the street immediately on his arrival.
It was reported in the newspapers that many ad-

dresses were found on him. This was not the case, however. True, a number of Bolsheviks were arrested at the same time, among these being Presyagin, who had just returned to Russia; but later this matter was cleared up. It appeared that in Leipzig, where Piatnitsky was working at that time on shipping literature to Russia and where Rykov stopped before his departure for Russia, there lived a certain Brendinsky, who transported the literature, in whom Piatnitsky and Mark had complete confidence. Later it was discovered that this Brendinsky was an *agent provocateur*. He coded the addresses for Rykov. This explains why the police were in possession of all the addresses although nothing was taken from Rykov when he was searched.

A conference was called in Baku. It was by mere accident that this conference was not raided by the police because one of the delegates of the conference, a well-known Baku worker named Stepan Shaumyan, was arrested together with a number of other Baku workers. The conference was transferred to Tiflis, where it was carried through successfully. Representatives were present from five organisations. Schwartz, Sergo and others were present. Bolsheviks and Plekhanovists were represented. Chernomazov who, later on, was proved to be an *agent provocateur*, was also there; but the Organisation Committee in Russia managed to complete its work—a Party conference was called in January 1912.

In 1911 the Bolshevik group in Paris was quite a strong organisation. It included Comrades Semashko, Vladimirsky, Antonov (Brittman), Kuznetsov (Sopozhkov), the Belinkys (Abram and his brother Grisha), Inessa, Stahl, Natasha Gopner, Kotlyarenko, Chernov (I do not remember his real name), Lenin, Zinoviev, Kamenev, Levina, Tarratuta, Mark (Liubimov), Lyova (Vladimirov), and others. In all, it had a membership of over forty. Taken on the whole, this group had considerable connection with Russia and much revolutionary experience.

The struggle against the liquidators, the Trotskyists and other opponents had hardened the group. It did a great deal to help the work in Russia, carried on a certain amount of work among the French workers, and among the masses of the emigrant Russian workers. There were quite a large number of these in Paris. At one time Comrade Stahl and I tried to carry on some work among the masses of foreign women workers—milliners, dressmakers, etc. We organised a number of meetings, but the importance of this work was not fully appreciated by our comrades and this was a great hindrance. At every meeting of the group someone would invariably raise a "racket": "Why call a woman's meeting?" they would say. And so the work petered out, although much good could have been done. Ilyich considered this work to be necessary.

At the end of September, Vladimir Ilyich went to Zurich to attend a conference of the International Socialist Bureau. At this meeting Molkenburg's letter to the Central Committee of the German Social-Democratic Party was discussed. In this letter Molkenburg averred that in view of the forthcoming elections, it would be inexpedient to criticise the German government's colonial policy in connection with the Morocco incidents. Rosa Luxemburg had secured a copy of this letter and published it. Bebel was indignant with her over this. Vladimir Ilyich defended Rosa. The opportunist policy pursued by the German Social-Democrats became clearly revealed at this meeting.

During this trip, Ilyich delivered a number of lectures in Switzerland.

In October the Lafargues committed suicide. Their death made a deep impression upon Ilyich. We recalled our visits to them. Ilyich said: "If one cannot work for the Party any longer, one must be able to look truth in the face and die like the Lafargues." And he felt a desire to say over their biers that their work had not been in vain; that the cause that they initiated, the cause of Marx, with which Paul and Laura Lafargue had been so closely associated, would grow and spread even to remote Asia. Just at that time the tide of revolution was rising in China. Vladimir Ilyich wrote out the speech and Inessa translated it. I remember with what deep emotion he delivered the speech at the funeral in the name of the Russian Social-Democratic Labour Party.

On the eve of the new year, the Bolsheviks called a conference of the Bolshevik groups abroad. Everyone was in good spirits, although life abroad had frayed everyone's nerves considerably.

BEGINNING OF 1912

Intensive preparations for the conference were being made. Vladimir Ilyich wrote to Nemetz, the Czech representative on the International Socialist Bureau, asking whether it would be possible to hold the conference in Prague. Prague was desirable because there was no Russian colony there and besides, Vladimir Ilyich knew Prague, for he had lived there in Modraczek's house in the period of his first exile.

I can recall two incidents in connection with the

Prague Conference (I was not present at the conference itself). One was the dispute between Savva (Zevin), the Ekaterinoslav delegate and formerly a student at the Longjumeau school, and the Kiev delegate, David (Schwartzman), and I think, also, Sergo. I can still picture Savva's excited face. I do not remember exactly what the dispute was about, but Savva was a Plekhanovist. Plekhanov did not go to the conference. "The make up of your conference," he wrote, in reply to the invitation, "is so uniform that it would be better, i.e. more in the interests of Party unity, if I kept away." But he had coached Savva as to the line he should take and at the conference the latter raised protest after protest in the spirit of Plekhanov. Later, as we know, Savva became a Bolshevik. The other Plekhanovist, David, sided with the Bolsheviks. I remember the circumstances in which the conversations were carried on at that time as to whether Savva should go to the conference or not. In Longjumeau Savva was always jolly and even-tempered, and that is why I was so surprised at this excitement at the conference.

The other incident was as follows. Vladimir Ilyich had already gone to Prague. Philip (Goloshchyokin) and Brendinsky arrived to go together to the conference. I knew Brendinsky only by name as a transporter of literature. He lived in Vilna, where Goloshchyokin also lived. His main function was to dispatch the literature received to the organisations, primarily to Moscow. He was registered on a false passport. Philip related that two weeks before the conference Brendinsky was arrested, that he was released after about ten days without any charge being brought against him, but that while he was in prison several people came to visit him who were afterwards arrested. He could not say exactly who it was that was arrested. I asked Philip to bring Brendinsky to me, but in the meantime not to tell him where the conference was to take place. The conversation with Brendinsky was a very strange one. We kept receiving word from Piatnitsky that the literature was being safely transported and delivered to Moscow and yet the comrades in Moscow were complaining that they were not receiving anything. The literature was addressed to Brendinsky, and so I asked him whether he could explain what became of this literature. He said that he had not delivered the literature to the organisation because it was very dangerous to do so, but that he had delivered it to some workers who were friends of his. I then asked him to give me their names. He mentioned several names but it was obvious that he had chosen them at random. He said that he did not remember their addresses. I began to question him about his journeys to various cities. I asked him something about a certain city, Yaroslav. He replied that he could not go there because he had been arrested there. "On what charge?" I asked. He answered, "On a criminal charge." I was dumbfounded. His answers became more and more confused. I then told him that the conference would be held in Brittany and that Ilyich and Zinoviev had already left for that place. Then Philip and I arranged that he and Gregory should go to Prague that night and leave a note for Brendinsky, saying that he had left for Brittany. I went to see Burtsev, who at that time specialised in detecting *agents provocateurs*. "There is no doubt that he's an *agent provocateur*," I said to Burtsev. He listened to what I had to say, and said: "Send him to me." There was no purpose, however, in sending the spy to Burtsev.

Later, Brendinsky's "artistry" was completely exposed. He never returned to Russia. The tsarist government bought him a villa in the suburbs of Paris for 40,000 francs.

I was very proud of the fact that I had saved the conference from an *agent provocateur*. I did not know, however, that there were two other *agents provocateurs* at the Prague conference, namely, Roman Malinovsky and Romanov (Alia Alexinsky, formerly a Capri student).

The Prague Conference was the first Party conference with workers from Russia that we succeeded in calling after 1908 and the first at which questions relating to the work in Russia were discussed in a businesslike manner and a definite line for this work drawn up. Resolutions were passed on the current situation and the tasks of the Party, on the elections to the Fourth Duma, on the work of the Social-Democratic fraction in the Duma, on the character and organisational forms of Party work, on the tasks of the Social-Democrats in the struggle against the famine which then raged in Russia, on the State Insurance for Workers' Bill that was before the Duma and on the petition campaign.*

A definite Party line on the questions of work in Russia; real leadership of *practical* work—these were the results of the Prague conference.

That is why the Prague conference was such an important one. At the conference a Central Committee was elected which included Lenin, Zinoviev, Ordjonikidze (Sergo), Schwartzman (David), Goloshchyokin (Philip), Spandarian and Malinovsky.

---

* A campaign organised by the liquidators and by Trotsky's organ *Pravda*, in December 1910, for collecting signatures for a petition to the "representatives of the people" in the Third Duma in favour of freedom of association for the workers.—Ed.

Substitutes were appointed who were to act, should any of the members be arrested. Soon after the conference, Stalin and Belostotsky (a student at the Longjumeau school) were co-opted to the Central Committee and so unity was established in the Central Committee, without which it would have been impossible to carry on the work during this trying time. The conference undoubtedly marked a great step forward: it checked the disintegration of the work in Russia. Relatively little importance was attached to the abusive attacks of the liquidators, to Trotsky, to Plekhanov's diplomacy, to the Bundists, etc. Although all this called for sharp resistance and exposure, they did not loom so large at this conference as at others. Attention was concentrated on the work in Russia. The misfortune was that Malinovsky was on the Central Committee, and all the details of the conference held with the representatives of the Third Duma—Poletaev and Shurkanov in Leipzig after the Prague conference, were also known to the police. Shurkanov, too, proved to be an *agent provocateur*. Undoubtedly, the *agent provocateur* sealed the fate of a number of Party workers and weakened the organisation; but the police were powerless to check the rise of the labour movement. The correct line laid down guided the movement into the right channel and created new forces in increasing number.

Ilyich went to Leipzig to confer with Poletaev and Shurkanov; after this he left for Berlin in order to obtain from the "trustees" the money they were holding and which was so greatly needed now for the work. Meanwhile Shotman came to visit us in Paris. He had been working in Finland just before that. The Prague Conference had passed a resolution strongly condemning the policy of the tsarist

government, and of the Third Duma towards Finland, and emphasising the need for unity between
the Finnish and Russian workers in the struggle
against tsarism and the Russian counter-revolutionary bourgeoisie. Our illegal organisation was
working in Finland at that time. Work was being
carried on among the sailors in the Baltic Fleet.
Shotman arrived to inform us that in Finland everything was ready for rebellion, that the illegal
organisation working among the Russian troops was
ready for battle (they were planning to seize the
Sveaborg and Kronstadt fortresses). Ilyich had not
yet returned. When he arrived, he questioned
Shotman closely about the organisation, the existence
of which was an interesting fact in itself (among the
comrades working in the organisation were Rakhya,
S. V. Vorobyev, and Kokko). He pointed out,
however, that it was inexpedient to start a rebellion
at that moment. It was very doubtful, he said,
whether the St. Petersburg workers would support
a rebellion just then. However, things never reached
the stage of rebellion. The organisation was discovered by the authorities, wholesale arrests took
place and fifty-two persons were tried on the charge
of conspiring to mutiny. Things were very remote
from rebellion, of course, but the shootings in the
Lena goldfields which occurred in the middle of
April, and the strikes that broke out all over the
country in protest against this outrage clearly revealed to what an extent the proletariat had developed during these years, revealed that the workers
had forgotten nothing, that the movement was rising
to a higher stage, that entirely new conditions of work
were arising.

Ilyich became another person, he became less
irritable, he concentrated more, pondered more on

the tasks which had arisen before the Russian labour movement—I should say that his mood at that time was best expressed in the article he wrote in memory of Hertzen in the beginning of May. In it he seemed to convey so much of himself, his ardent passion which fascinated and gripped one so. He wrote: "In honouring the memory of Hertzen, we clearly see three generations, the three classes which have been active in the Russian revolution. First—the nobility and landlords, the Decembrists and Hertzen. This group of revolutionaries was a restricted one. They were frightfully remote from the people. But the cause for which they fought was not lost. The Decembrists roused Hertzen. Hertzen developed revolutionary agitation.

"This agitation was taken up, broadened, strengthened, and steeled by the revolutionary 'rasnochintsi,'* beginning with Chernishevsky and ending with the heroes of the *Narodnaya Volya* (*Peoples' Will*). The circle of these fighters broadened and their contacts with the people became more intimate. Hertzen called them 'young pilots in the coming storm.' That was not yet the real storm.

"The storm—that is the movement of the masses themselves. The proletariat, the only really consistent revolutionary class rose and became the leader of the masses and for the first time roused millions of peasants for the open revolutionary struggle. The storm first broke in 1905. The second outburst is developing before our very eyes."

Only a few months before that, Vladimir Ilyich had said to Anna Ilyinishna, who had arrived in Paris: "I do not know whether I will live to see the next rise of the tide." But now he sensed the

* Those middle-class elements of the intelligentsia who did not belong to any of the officially recognised "estates."

gathering storm, the movement of the masses themselves, with every fibre of his being.

When the first number of *Pravda* came out we began to make preparations to move to Cracow. Cracow was in many respects more convenient than Paris. It was more convenient in regard to the police. The French police assisted the Russian police in every possible way. The Polish police, however, was hostile to the Russian police as it was in fact to the whole of the Russian government. In Cracow we could be sure that our letters would not be intercepted and that no one would spy on newcomers. Moreover, the Russian frontier was very close and it was easier to get to and from Russia. Letters and parcels could be sent to Russia without trouble. We hurriedly made preparations to depart. Vladimir Ilyich became quite jolly and particularly solicitous for the welfare of the comrades who were to remain behind. Crowds and crowds of people came to see us. I remember Kurnatovsky came. We knew him from our exile together in Shusha. That had been the third time he was in exile. He was a graduate of the Zurich university. He was a chemical engineer by profession and worked in a sugar refinery near Minusinsk. Soon after his return to Russia he was again arrested in Tiflis and spent two years in the military prison in the Metekh fortress, after which he was sent to Yakutsk. On his way there he got involved in the "Romanov affair"* and was sentenced to twelve years' penal servitude. In 1905 he was

---

* In 1904 the political exiles in Yakutsk, in the extreme north-east of Russia, rose in armed rebellion against the inhuman treatment to which they were subjected. They blockaded themselves in the house of a Yakut named Romanov, where they were besieged by tsarist forces for eighteen days. Finally, the rebels surrendered after a pitched battle lasting three days. They were tried and sentenced to twelve years' penal servitude.—Ed.

amnestied. He organised the "Chita Republic,"* was captured by General Meller-Zakomelsky and handed over to General Rennenkampf. He was sentenced to death and taken for a ride in the punitive train so that he could see the revolutionaries being shot by the firing squads along the railway line. Later, his sentence was commuted to exile for life. In 1906 he succeeded in escaping from Nerchinsk to Japan. From there he made his way to Australia, where he lived in dire poverty. At one time he worked as a lumber-jack, caught a chill, got an inflammation in one of his ears and generally was reduced to a state of exhaustion. With great difficulty he made his way to Paris. His end was a sad one indeed. In the autumn of 1910 Ilyich and I used to visit him in hospital. He suffered from terrible pains in the head. Ekaterina Ivanovna Okulova also visited him with her little daughter who used to write notes to him in her childish hand, because he was almost deaf and could not hear what she said. He recovered somewhat later and became involved with the conciliators. In a conversation one day he started to talk like the conciliators and our friendship with him began to cool off. We were all very highly strung. I visited him one day in the autumn of 1911. He was then living in a small room on the Boulevard Montparnasse. I brought him our newspapers, told him about the school at Longjumeau and we had a long heart-to-heart talk. He then unreservedly agreed with the line of the Central Committee. Ilyich was very glad to hear this and began to visit him frequently. Kurnatovsky watched us pack our things for our journey to Cracow. Noting how joyfully my

* At that time a wave of rebellion swept over Siberia. In Chita the rebels seized the town and established a short-lived "Republic."— Ed.

mother was packing her things he said: "Why, some people have got energy!" In the autumn of 1912, when we were already in Cracow, Kurnatovsky died.

We sublet our apartment to a Pole, a Cracow precentor, who took the apartment with the furniture. He made many inquiries of Ilyich about household affairs; "What's the price of geese?" he asked; "How much is veal?" Ilyich did not know what to answer. "Geese??" "Veal??" Ilyich knew very little about household affairs, but even I could not tell him anything about geese and veal, for during our stay in Paris we had not eaten either the one or the other. Had the precentor interested himself in the price of horse-flesh and lettuce I could have told him.

All our people in Paris at that time longed terribly to go to Russia: there were Inessa, Safarov and others. We were only moving a little nearer to Russia.

CRACOW
(1912-14)

Exile in Cracow was unlike that in Paris or Switzerland. In fact it was semi-exile. In Cracow we were almost entirely absorbed in the work in Russia. Close connections with Russia were very quickly established. Newspapers from St. Petersburg would arrive only three days old. At this time, *Pravda* was being published in Russia. "And in Russia the *revolutionary* revival is not any kind of a revival, but a revolutionary revival," Ilyich wrote to Gorki. "And we did after all succeed in establishing a daily *Pravda*—thanks, incidentally, to the very (January) conference which fools are abusing." Very close

contacts were established with *Pravda*. Ilyich wrote
articles for it almost every day, sent letters, watched
it carefully and recruited contributors for it. He tried
hard to persuade Maxim Gorki to write for it.
Zinoviev also wrote regularly for the paper and
collected interesting material on foreign affairs for it.
Such systematic collaboration would have been impossible from Paris and Switzerland. Correspondence was also soon established. The Cracow comrades taught us how to arrange things more secretly.
The important thing was to see to it that letters did
not bear foreign post-marks. Thus, the Russian
police paid no attention to them. Peasant women
from Russia would come to market in Cracow and
for a small fee would take our letters across and drop
them into the letter-boxes in Russia.

About 4,000 Polish exiles lived in Cracow.

When we arrived in Cracow, we were met by Comrade Bagotsky—a Polish political exile, who immediately took us under his charge and helped us with
our everyday and secret work. He taught us how
to make use of the "polupaska" (or semi-passport;
this was the term applied to the permits to cross the
frontier given to the local inhabitants on either
side). The "polupaska" cost very little and above all
they greatly facilitated the work of our illegal comrades in crossing to and from Russia. Many comrades crossed into Russia with the aid of these permits. Varvara Nikolayevna Yakovleva was smuggled
through in this way. She had been in exile in Siberia,
where she contracted tuberculosis. She escaped from
Siberia in order to get medical treatment and to see
her brother in Germany. After a time, she went back
to Russia and stopped in Cracow in order to make
arrangements for maintaining correspondence and
organising the work in Russia. She got through

quite safely. Only quite recently I learned that on crossing the frontier the gendarmes were attracted by the large trunk which she carried and wanted to know whether she was really going to the destination indicated on her ticket. But the car attendant warned her about this, and for a price she consented to buy her ticket to Warsaw. In this way she got to her destination without mishap. Once we got Stalin across that way. On the frontier the names of the passengers are called and each had to answer in Polish, "present." I remember that I tried to teach this little wisdom to our comrades. Soon after we organised the crossing of the frontier illegally, i.e. by smuggling the comrades across. On the Russian side addresses to which the comrades could go were supplied by Comrade Krylenko* who lived in Lublin not far from the frontier at that time. In this way we were also able to smuggle illegal literature across. I must say that in Cracow the police did not spy on us, they did not intercept our correspondence and, generally speaking, they had no contact with the Russian police. On one occasion we were able to convince ourselves of this. One day, Shumkin, a Moscow worker, came to us for literature which he wanted to smuggle through in the form of a sort of breast-plate (a specially made waistcoat filled with literature). He was a great conspirator and used to walk about the street with his cap pulled low over his forehead. We went to a meeting and asked him to go with us. He agreed but refused to walk together with us because he thought this would be risky, but followed at some distance behind us. The look of the obvious conspirator about him attracted the attention of the Cracow police. Next

* Until recently, Chief Public Prosecutor of the U.S.S.R. and now Commissar of Justice of the U.S.S.R.—Ed.

day a police officer called on us and asked
whether we knew the man and whether we could
vouch for him. We assured him that we could.
Shumkin, however, insisted on taking the literature
in spite of the fact that the police had their eye
on him. We tried to dissuade him from doing so,
but he insisted and smuggled the literature through
safely.

We arrived in Cracow in the summer and Comrade Bagotsky advised us to move to the suburb of
Zvezhintsa where we rented a house together with
the Zinovievs. The streets in this district were un-
paved and exceedingly muddy. But the river
Vistula was quite near in which we were able to
bathe, and about five kilometres away there was the
"Volsky Lyas," a beautiful wood which Ilyich and I
frequently visited on our bicycles. In the autumn we
moved to the other end of the town, a newly built
section. Bagotsky and the Zinovievs moved there
with us.

Ilyich liked Cracow very much; it reminded him
of Russia. The change of environment, the absence
of emigré squabbles soothed our nerves somewhat.
Ilyich carefully observed the everyday life of the
Cracow population, its poverty and its workers. I,
too, liked Cracow. I lived in Poland when I was a
child from the age of two to five, something of it still
remained in my memory, and so the wide verandas,
looking on to the courtyard, appealed to me for they
reminded me of the verandas on the steps of which
I used to play with the Polish and Jewish children
when I was a child. I liked the little gardens where
sour milk and potatoes were sold. This reminded
my mother also of her young days. And Ilyich was
very happy that he had escaped from Paris at last.
He was in a merry mood and would jokingly praise

G

the sour milk and the Polish "motsna starka" (a strong corn whisky).

Lilina could speak Polish better than any of us. I could speak it a little; I remembered some of it from childhood and had studied the language while in Siberia and Ufa and I had to speak Polish in my housekeeping affairs. Housekeeping was a much more serious business here than in Paris. There was no gas and we were compelled to light the stove every day. At the butcher's I asked for meat without bones, as it is sold in Paris. The butcher glared at me and answered: "The Lord God created cows with bones, so how can you expect me to sell you meat without bones?" We had to provide ourselves with bread for Mondays in advance, because on Mondays the bakers would be getting over the effects of "the night before" and the bakeries would be closed. One had to be able to haggle with the market women. There were Polish stores and Jewish stores. In the Jewish stores one could buy things ever so much cheaper than at the others, but one had to haggle over the price, to pretend to leave the shop in disgust and be called back by the shop-keeper.

The Jews lived in a separate quarter of the town and dressed differently from the rest of the inhabitants. In waiting-rooms of hospitals one could hear the patients, while waiting to see the doctor, seriously discussing whether Jewish children were exactly like Polish children. Once I heard such a conversation and close by there stood a little Jewish boy who overheard it all. The power of the Catholic clergy—of the priests, was boundless in Cracow. They engaged in philanthropic work and gave assistance to those whose house had been burned down, to aged women and to orphans; the convents organised registry offices for domestic servants and saw that they were not ill-treated by their mistresses. Going to church was the only recreation the down-trodden, ignorant population enjoyed. In Galicia feudal customs were still rife and were fostered by the Catholic Church. For example, a lady would come to the market to hire a servant. About a dozen peasant women who had come to the market to hire themselves as servants would surround the lady and would all kiss her hand. Tips were expected for all services. A carpenter or a coachman, on receiving a tip, would get down on his hands and knees and bow his head to the ground. But in spite of all this, the masses were filled with hatred for their masters. The nursemaid whom the Zinovievs had hired for their little boy would go to church every morning. She was positively emaciated as a result of all the fasting and praying. When I talked to her she told me that she hated the masters, that once she had worked for three years for the wife of an officer who, like all ladies, would sleep until eleven o'clock, would take her coffee in bed and compelled her servants to dress her and pull on her stockings. This fanatic-ally religious nursemaid said that if a revolution broke out, she would be the first one to take a pitchfork and go against the masters. The poverty and wretch-edness of the peasants and of the poor generally was evident all around and was still greater than in Russia at that time.

In Cracow, Vladimir Ilyich met Comrade Gan-etsky, who had been a delegate of the Social-Demo-cratic Party of Poland and Lithuania to the Second Congress and later acted as delegate of the Manage-ment Committee to the Stockholm and London Congresses. From Comrade Ganetsky and other Polish comrades, Vladimir Ilyich learned the par-

ticulars of the split which had occurred among the
Polish Social-Democrats. The Management Committee started a campaign against the Warsaw Committee which had the support of the entire Warsaw
organisation. The Warsaw Committee demanded
that the Management Committee pursue a line in
keeping with strict principles and take up a more
definite position on the internal Party affairs of the
Russian Social-Democratic Labour Party. The
Management Committee dissolved the Warsaw
Committee and began to spread rumours to the effect
that the latter had connections with the secret police.
Vladimir Ilyich took the side of the Warsaw Committee. He wrote an article in which he defended
them, and also wrote to the International Socialist
Bureau protesting against the conduct of the
Management Committee. The Warsaw Committee
was closely connected with the masses in Warsaw
and in other industrial centres (Lodz, etc.). Ilyich
did not regard the fight of the "Rozlamovists," or
Dissidents as the Warsaw Committee was called, to
be an extraneous affair, but as an important part
of the general struggle within the Party, so acute at
the time. Hence, he could not remain a mere on-
looker. Nevertheless, his attention was mainly
absorbed in Russian affairs.

Safarov and Inessa, close comrades, went from
Paris to St. Petersburg to make preparations for
the election campaign. They travelled with other
people's passports. Inessa stopped at Cracow and
visited us in Zvezhintsa and stayed with us for two
days. We discussed all the arrangements with her
and supplied her with addresses and connections.
She and Ilyich discussed the whole plan of work. On
her way, Inessa was to call on Nikolai Vasilievich
Krylenko, who lived in Lublin in Poland not far

from the Galician border, in order to discuss with him the arrangements for enabling comrades coming to Cracow to cross the frontier. Inessa and Safarov sent us a great deal of information about what was going on in St. Petersburg. After establishing connections there, they did a great deal of work in informing the Party workers of the resolutions passed at the Prague Conference and discussing with them the problems which then faced the Party. They established their base in the Narva district of St. Petersburg. They restored the St. Petersburg Committee of the Party and later formed the Northern Regional Bureau of which Inessa and Safarov, as well as Shotman and his comrades, Rakhya and Pravdin, were members. A very acute fight was raging in St. Petersburg against the liquidators. The Northern Regional Bureau prepared the ground for the election of Badayev, a Bolshevik and railwayman by trade, as deputy for St. Petersburg. The liquidators were losing their influence over the masses of the St. Petersburg workers who realised that instead of carrying on a revolutionary struggle the liquidators had taken the road of reform and were actually pursuing a liberal-labour policy. A determined struggle had to be waged against the liquidators. That is why Vladimir Ilyich was so upset when *Pravda* at first deliberately struck out from his articles all his arguments in opposition to the liquidators. He wrote angry letters to *Pravda* protesting against this. Only gradually did *Pravda* join in the struggle. The police, too, had made all preparations for the elections. On the fourteenth, Inessa and Safarov were arrested. But the police had not yet discovered Stalin, who had escaped from exile and had arrived on the twelfth. The elections of the workers' curia* passed off quite successfully. Not a single candidate of the Right was elected. At all meetings resolutions of a political character were passed.

During the month of October, all attention was concentrated on the elections. In many districts the workers, owing to their ignorance and inertia, were indifferent to the elections and did not attach much importance to them, and so wide agitation had to be carried on in order to arouse their interest. Nevertheless, the workers everywhere elected Social-Democrats. The elections in all the six workers' curia of the largest industrial centres resulted in a Bolshevik victory. Workers, members of the Party, who enjoyed great authority among their fellow workers, were elected. Six Bolsheviks and seven Menshevik deputies were elected to the Duma, but the six Bolshevik deputies represented a million workers, whereas the seven Menshevik deputies represented less than a quarter of a million workers. Moreover, from the very beginning, the Bolshevik group was distinguished for its discipline and solidarity. The opening of the Duma on October 18th was accompanied by workers' demonstrations and strikes. The Bolshevik deputies had to work in the Duma in conjunction with the Mensheviks. Meanwhile, the internal Party differences became more acute. In January the Prague Conference took place which played an important part in organising the Bolshevik forces.

* The elections to the Duma were indirect, i.e. the electors did not vote directly for the members of the Duma, but for "electors" who formed a "curia" as it was called, which in turn voted for the members of the electoral college which finally elected the members of the Duma. The curia were elected according to the social category of the voters, for example, landlords, peasants, urban middle class and workers, each category having its own curia.—Ed.

Towards the end of August 1912 a so-called Party Conference was convened in Vienna on the initiative and with the active participation of Trotsky. The object of this conference was stated to be, to unite all the Social-Democratic forces, but the degree to which the roads of the liquidators and the Bolsheviks had diverged and the fact that the conduct of the liquidators was in complete variance with the Party line, were completely ignored. The *Vperyod*-ists were also invited to this conference. It could have been said in advance that the conference would bear a purely liquidationist character. Not only did the Bolsheviks, who supported the Central Committee, stay away from this conference, but so also did the Menshevik Plekhanovists and the Bolshevik conciliators who were grouped around Plekhanov's magazine *Za Partiu* (*For the Party*), which was published abroad. The Poles, too, stayed away and Alexinsky, who was sent to the conference by the *Vperyod* group, exposed the one-sided character of the conference. The great majority of the delegates of the conference were persons who lived abroad; two Caucasian delegates were sent to represent the Caucasian Regional Bureau; on the whole, all the delegates were elected by very small groups. The resolutions passed by the conference were of a pronounced liquidationist character. The slogan of a democratic republic was deleted from the election platform; the slogan of "revision of the agrarian law of the Third Duma" was substituted for the slogan of "confiscation of the landlords' estates."

Boris Goldman (Gorev), one of the principal speakers at the conference, declared that the old Party no longer existed and that the present conference must become an "inaugural" conference. Even Alexinsky protested against this. This amalgamation of compromises, the August *bloc*, as it became known, set itself in opposition to the Central Committee and tried to discredit the decisions of the Prague Conference. Under the cloak of unity, unity against the Bolsheviks was established.

Meanwhile, the labour movement in Russia was rising. This was proved by the elections.

Soon after the elections, Comrade Muranov, a member of the Duma, visited us. He crossed the border illegally. Ilyich was shocked at this. "What a scandal there would have been," he said to Muranov, "if you had been caught! You are a member of the Duma and enjoy parliamentary immunity; you would have suffered no harm had you come legally. You might have caused a scandal by the way you came." Muranov related many interesting events about the elections in Kharkov, about his Party work, how he got his wife to distribute leaflets when she went to market with him, etc. Muranov was an inveterate conspirator and he simply could not understand what "parliamentary immunity" meant. Ilyich talked with him about future work in the Duma and urged him to go back as quickly as possible. After this, members of the Duma would visit us openly.

The first conference with the members of the Duma took place at the end of December and the beginning of January.

Malinovsky* arrived first. He seemed to be very excited about something. I did not like him at first, his eyes seemed unpleasant to me and I did not like his affected ease; but this impression passed off after the first serious conversation we had with him. Then Petrovsky and Badayev† arrived. The deputies told us about their first month's work in the Duma and

---

* Later proved to have been a spy.—Ed.

† Author of *The Bolsheviks in the Tsarist Duma*.—Ed.

about their work among the masses. I can even now recall Badayev standing in the doorway waving his cap and saying: "Why the masses have grown up enormously during these last few years!" Malinovsky gave one the impression of being a very intelligent and influential worker. Badayev and Petrovsky were shy, but it was quite obvious that they were good, reliable proletarians. At this conference, the plan of work was drawn up, the character of the speeches to be delivered in the Duma, the character of the work to be carried on among the masses and the question of closely linking up this work with the illegal activity of the Party were discussed. The work of supervising *Pravda* was assigned to Badayev. Comrade Medvedev arrived with the Duma deputies. He told us about his work of printing leaflets. Ilyich was quite pleased. "Malinovsky, Petrovsky and Badayev," he wrote to Gorki on January 1st, 1913, "send you their hearty greetings and best wishes. The Cracow base has proved useful: our coming to Cracow has proved quite worth-while (from the point of view of the cause)."

In the autumn the "great powers" intervened in the Balkan affair, and things began to smack of war. The International Socialist Bureau organised protest meetings everywhere. A meeting was also held in Cracow, but here they bore a rather peculiar character. It was more like a meeting called to rouse the hatred of the masses towards Russia than a protest meeting against war.

The International Socialist Bureau arranged to call a special congress of the Socialist International at Basle on November 11th and 12th. Kamenev was sent to this congress as representative of the Central Committee of the Russian Social-Democratic Labour Party.

Vladimir Ilyich was indignant at an article written by Kautsky in *Neue Zeit*. This article was thoroughly opportunistic, and in it Kautsky argued that it would be a mistake for the workers to organise armed uprisings and strikes against war. Vladimir Ilyich had already written a great deal about the organising rôle strikes played in the revolution of 1905. After the publication of Kautsky's article he dealt with this question at greater length in a series of articles. He attached enormous importance to strikes as well as all other forms of direct action on the part of the masses.

At the Stuttgart Congress, 1907, five years before the Basle Congress, the question of war was discussed and outlined in the spirit of revolutionary Marxism. During the intervening five years, opportunism had made enormous strides. Kautsky's article was a striking illustration of this. However, the Basle Congress unanimously adopted the manifesto against war and a huge mass anti-war demonstration was organised. Only in 1914 was the extent to which the Second International had been corroded by opportunism really revealed.

During the Cracow period, i.e. the years immediately preceding the outbreak of the imperialist war, Vladimir Ilyich devoted a great deal of attention to the national question. Since his early youth, he had hated national oppression in every form. Marx's statement that no greater misfortune can befall a nation than that it subdue another nation, was near and comprehensible to him.

War was approaching. The national spirit of the bourgeoisie was rising. The bourgeoisie tried to rouse national passion and hatred in every possible way. The approaching war bore with it the increased oppression of weak nationalities and the suppression of their independence. But the war would inevitably—Ilyich had no doubts about this, develop into rebellion; the oppressed nationalities would fight for their independence. This was their right. The International Socialist Congress held in London in 1896 had already confirmed this right. The under-estimation of the right of nations to self-determination at such a time, the end of 1912 and beginning of 1913, in the face of impending war, filled Vladimir Ilyich with indignation. Not only had the August bloc failed to rise to the heights demanded by the situation, not only did it fail to bring this question out more sharply, but it even passed a resolution to the effect that cultural, national autonomy (concerning which a controversy had raged even in 1903 at the Second Party Congress and which was voted down at the time) was compatible with the point in the Party programme which demanded the right of nations to self-determination. This was tantamount to surrendering the position on the national question and to restricting the whole struggle to the struggle for culture as if it were not obvious that culture was bound by a thousand threads to the political system. Ilyich regarded this as opportunism carried to the utmost extreme. But the most serious controversy on the question of the right of nations to self-determination was carried on with the Poles. The latter—Rosa Luxemburg and the "Rozlamovists" maintained that the right of nations to self-determination does not necessarily mean the establishment of separate states. Ilyich appreciated the reasons why the Poles were disturbed on the question of the right to self-determination. The Polish masses were filled with burning hatred against tsarism—this manifested itself daily in Cracow: one remembered what

his father had experienced during the Polish rebellion, and that he had barely escaped from the
gallows; another remembered how the tsarist
authorities desecrated the graves of his nearest and
dearest by letting pigs into the cemetery, etc., etc.
Russian tsarism not only oppressed the Poles, but
mocked at and humiliated them.

War was approaching, and with it was rising not
only Black Hundred nationalism, not only the
chauvinism of the bourgeoisie of the ruling states,
but also the hopes of emancipation of the oppressed
nationalities. The Polish Socialist Party was dreaming more and more about the independence of
Poland. The growing separatist tendencies of the
Polish Socialist Party—the Party was thoroughly
petty-bourgeois—caused alarm among the Polish
Social-Democrats. The Polish Social-Democrats
were opposed to Poland's secession from Russia.
Ilyich met members of the Polish Socialist Party.
Several times he had talks with one of their best
workers, Jodko, and he heard Dashinsky speak. He
was, therefore, able to understand what was dis-
turbing the Poles. "But we cannot approach the
question of the right of nations to self-determination
only from the point of view of the Poles!"—he would
say.

The controversy on the national question which
had arisen as early as the second congress of our
Party became particularly acute on the eve of the
war in 1913-14 and continued in 1916 when the
imperialist war was at its height. In these disputes
Ilyich played a leading part. The controversy
proved to be very useful for it helped our Party to
solve the national problem in the Soviet state when
it was established by creating the Union of Soviet
Socialist Republics in which all nationalities are

equal and the rights of none are restricted. In our country we see the rapid cultural development of the nationalities which formerly had lived under unbearable oppression. We see unity between the nationalities in the U.S.S.R. becoming closer and closer. In the U.S.S.R. numerous nationalities are united by the common ties of socialist construction.

It would be a mistake to think, however, that the national question which occupied Ilyich during the Cracow period made him forget such questions as the peasant question to which he always attached very great significance. During the Cracow period, Vladimir Ilyich wrote over forty articles on the peasant question. He wrote a detailed memorandum *On the Question of the Agrarian Policy (general) of the Present Government* for the Duma deputy, Shagov, and a speech *On the Question of the Estimates of the Department of Agriculture* for the Duma deputy, G. I. Petrovsky. In Cracow he began writing his big work, *New Data On the Laws of Development of Capitalism in Agriculture*, based on a study of American data. America is famous for the efficiency and wealth of her statistics. In this work Lenin set out to refute the views of Himmer (the name of the now notorious Sukhanov, one of the leading figures in the Menshevik wreckers' conspiracy case tried in 1931). Concerning him, Vladimir Ilyich wrote: "Himmer is not a casual writer of casual newspaper articles, but an outstanding economist who represents the more democratic, extreme 'Left' *bourgeois* trend in Russian and European public opinion. This is precisely why the opinions of Mr. Himmer are likely to have—and on the non-proletarian sections of the population they already have to some extent—particularly wide influence. For these are not his own personal views, not his own errors; they are the especially democratised, the especially embellished with alleged socialist phraseology, expression of *general bourgeois* ideas, which, under the capitalist system of society, the official professor who treads the beaten track and the small farmer who is conspicuous for his intelligence among the millions of his kind, can best appreciate.

The theory of non-capitalist evolution of agriculture under the capitalist system of society, which Mr. Himmer advocates, is, in reality, the theory adhered to by the great majority of bourgeois professors, of bourgeois democrats and of opportunists in the labour movement throughout the world."

This book was completed in 1915 but it was not published before 1917.

Eight years after he had completed this book, in 1923, when Ilyich was already sick, he perused Sukhanov's memoirs of the revolution and dictated an article on them which was published in *Pravda* under the heading "About Our Revolution." In this article he wrote: "Now there is no longer any doubt about the fact that in the main, we have achieved victory." Sukhanov failed to understand this. Ilyich went on to say in this article: "During the past day or two, I have been perusing Sukhanov's memoirs of the revolution. What strikes one about them is the pedantry that is characteristic of all our petty-bourgeois democrats as well as of all the heroes of the Second International. . . . Apart from the fact that they are exceedingly cowardly . . . it is their slavish support of the past that is so conspicuous. . . . They all call themselves Marxists, but their understanding of Marx is hopelessly pedantic. The most important point in Marxism, namely, his revolutionary dialectics, they have completely failed to understand. . . . In all their conduct they prove themselves to be cowardly reformists who fear to take one step away from the bourgeoisie, let alone break with them completely." Then he goes on to say that the world imperialist war created conditions "in which we were able to achieve precisely that alliance between the 'peasant war' and the labour movement which a 'Marxist' like Marx suggested as one of the prospects for Russia in 1856."

Eight more years have passed since then. Ilyich is no longer among us, and still Sukhanov fails to understand the conditions the October Revolution has created for building Socialism and actively strives to hinder the work of eradicating the remnants of capitalism; he does not realise how the face of our country has changed. Collective and state farms are growing and becoming consolidated. Tractors are ploughing up virgin soil. The old unploughed strips that served as the dividing lines between the innumerable small peasant plots are a thing of the past; labour is being organised on modern lines; the entire aspect of agriculture has changed.

In the numerous articles he wrote during the Cracow period Ilyich dealt with a number of extremely important questions connected with peasant and landlord farming in which he gave a strikingly clear picture of the situation in this sphere at the time, outlined the agrarian programmes of the various parties and exposed the character of the government measures and called attention to a number of problems of extreme importance, for example, colonisation, wage labour in agriculture, child labour, the buying and selling of land, the concentration of peasant lands, etc. Ilyich knew the countryside and the needs of the peasants very well indeed, and both the workers and the peasants realised this.

The rise of the revolutionary labour movement at the end of 1912 and the rôle which *Pravda* played in this was obvious to all, even to the *Vperyod*-ists.

In November 1912 Alexinsky applied to the editorial board of *Pravda* in the name of the Paris group of the *Vperyod*-ists offering their co-operation. Alexinsky wrote a number of articles for *Pravda* and in No. 3 of the *Vperyod*-ist magazine *Na Temi Dnya* (*Current Topics*) he even urged the necessity for putting a stop to the internal struggle within the Bolshevik ranks and the necessity for forming a bloc to include all the Bolsheviks for the purpose of fighting against the liquidators. The editorial board of *Pravda* not only included members of the Paris group like Alexinsky in its list of contributors, but also Bogdanov. Ilyich learned of this only through the press. One of Ilyich's characteristic traits was his ability to distinguish disputes on principles from personal disputes and his ability to place the interests of the cause above everything else. Even if Plekhanov did pour abuse on him, if the interests of the cause demanded that he should unite with him, Ilyich did not hesitate to do so. Even if Alexinsky did break his way into a meeting of the group and behave in a disgraceful manner,—but since he had realised that it was necessary to work whole-heartedly for the *Pravda*, to fight the liquidators, to fight for the Party, Ilyich was sincerely glad. Many similar examples could be given. When an opponent attacked him, Ilyich was roused, he hit back, pressed his own point of view; but when new tasks arose and it was found possible to co-operate with the opponent, Ilyich was able to approach the opponent of yesterday as a comrade. He did not have to force himself to do this, it came naturally. Herein lay Ilyich's tremendous power. For all his jealousy touching

questions of principle, he was a great optimist as far
as persons were concerned. He would sometimes
err, but on the whole this optimism was very bene-
ficial for the cause. But if agreement could not be
reached on matters of principle, then there was no
reconciliation.

In a letter to Gorki, Ilyich wrote: "I am ready
with all my heart to share your joy at the return of
the *Vperyod*-ists, that is, *if* . . . *if* your supposition
that Machism, god-creating, and all that stuff are
really, as you say, a thing of the past. If that really
is the case, if the *Vperyod*-ists have realised, or will
realise this now, then I heartily join you in your
joy at their return. But I emphasise the '*if*,' because so far, it is more a wish than a fact. . . . I do not
know whether Bogdanov, Bazarov, Volsky (a semi-
anarchist), Lunacharsky and Alexinsky are *capable
of learning* a lesson from the trying experiences of the
years 1908-11. Have they learned that Marxism is
something more serious and more profound than they
thought, that one cannot mock at it as Alexinsky did,
or scorn it as a dead object, as others did. *If* they
have realised that—a thousand greetings to them and
all personal things (which inevitably arise in acute
struggles) will disappear in a twinkling. However, if
they have not realised this, if they have not learned
the lesson, then don't blame me: friendship is friendship, and duty is duty. We will fight to the death
against any attempt to throw mud at Marxism or to
confuse the policy of the workers' party.

" I am very glad that a *road* has been found for a
gradual return of the *Vperyod*-ists via *Pravda*, which
did not attack them directly. I am very glad. But
for the sake of a more *durable* friendship, we must
approach it slowly, cautiously. I have said the same
thing in *Pravda*. The friends who are anxious to

H

bring about a reunion between us and the *Vperyod*-ists must also concentrate their efforts on this: a cautious *return* of the *Vperyod*-ists, tested by experience, from Machism, Otzovism and god-creating can do a devil of a lot of good. The slightest carelessness, however, may cause a relapse to Machism, Otzovism, etc.—and a more bitter struggle than ever is likely to flare up. . . . I have not read Bogdanov's *Philosophy of Living Experience*; very likely it is the old, mechanistic philosopher in a new garb."

Reading these lines now, one vividly recalls the whole path of struggle and the whole of that period of disruption between 1908 and 1911. When that period had passed and Ilyich had become completely absorbed in Russian work and was carried away by the growing revival of the movement, he could speak more calmly about the *Vperyod*-ists, but he hardly believed, or to be more correct, he did not believe at all that Alexinsky was capable of learning from experience and that Bogdanov would give up Machism. Things turned out exactly as Ilyich anticipated. An open conflict soon broke out with Bogdanov who, on the pretext of popularising the word "ideology" attempted to drag his philosophy into *Pravda*. Things finally reached the point where Bogdanov was removed from the list of contributors to *Pravda*.

In the Cracow period Vladimir Ilyich's thoughts were already directed towards socialist construction. Of course, this can only be said in a conventional sense, for at that time the direction the socialist revolution in Russia would take was not yet clear. Nevertheless, had we not experienced the Cracow period of semi-exile at a time when the leadership of political struggle of the Duma fraction required the concrete handling of questions of economic and cultural life, it would have been difficult, in the period immediately following the October revolution, to deal with all the aspects of Soviet construction that arose. It was sort of a "standard O" (preparatory class) for socialist construction. Of course at first, Ilyich merely presented these problems in rough outline, but they were so vivid that they hold good even to-day.

During this time Vladimir Ilyich devoted considerable attention to questions of culture. At the end of December, arrests and raids occurred in St. Petersburg among the students of the Vitmer Gymnasium.* The Vitmer Gymnasium was, of course, different from other gymnasiums. The head mistress and her husband took an active part in the first Marxist study circles that were formed in the 'nineties. In 1905-07 they rendered considerable service to the Bolsheviks. In the Vitmer Gymnasium the students were permitted to participate in political life, to form political circles, etc. And so the police raided this gymnasium. An interpellation was made in the Duma concerning the arrest of the students. The Minister for Education, Kasso, gave an explanation. His explanation was rejected as unsatisfactory by a majority of votes. In an article entitled "Increasing Discrepancies," written for Nos. 3 and 4 of *Prosveshchenie* (*Education*) in 1913, Vladimir Ilyich in Chapter 10 stated that in connection with the arrests of the students of the Vitmer Gymnasium, the Duma passed a vote of no confidence in Kasso, the Minister for Education. But this, he says, is not the only thing that people should know. "The people and the democracy must know the *reasons* for this lack of confidence in order to *understand* the causes of what is regarded as abnormal in politics,

* High School.—Ed.

and in order to be able to find *a way* to the normal."
He then goes on to examine the manner in which the
various parties in the Duma formulated their motion
"to proceed to the order of the day."* After examining the manner in which the Social-Democrats
formulated their motion, Ilyich goes on to say:
"Even this formula cannot be regarded as faultless.
We cannot but wish that it were drafted in a more
popular and clearer style; we cannot but regret that
it did not point out the legality of engaging in politics,
etc., etc. But our criticism of *all the formulae* is not in
the least directed against the manner in which they
were drafted, but is directed exclusively against the
political ideas of their authors. The main thing a
democrat should have said was: that circles and discussion are *natural and should be welcomed*. That is the
point. All condemnation of political activity even
'at an early age' is hypocrisy and obscurantism. A
democrat should have raised the question from that
of a 'united cabinet' to that of the political régime.
A democrat should have pointed out the 'indissoluble
connection' firstly 'with the domination of the secret
police', secondly with the domination of the class of
big landlords of the feudal type in economic life."

This is how Vladimir Ilyich taught how to link
up concrete questions of culture with important
political questions.

In speaking about culture, Ilyich always empha-
sised the connection between culture and the general
political and economic system. In protesting resolutely against this slogan of cultural-national autonomy, Ilyich wrote: "As long as different nationalities
live under a single state they are bound together by
millions and billions of threads of an economic
juridical and social character. How can we exclude

* Similar to: move the adjournment of the House.—Ed.

education from these ties? Can education be 're-moved from the sphere of control' of the state, as that classical example of absurdity, the formula of the Bund, puts it? If economics unite nations who live under a single state then the attempt to divide them once and for all in the sphere of 'culture,' and particularly on questions of education, is absurd and reactionary. On the contrary, we strive to *unite* the nations in the sphere of education in order that the school may prepare for what is carried out in life. At present we see the inequality of nations and un-evenness in their level of development; under such conditions the division of education according to nationality will indeed be a handicap for the more backward nations. In the Southern States in America which were formerly slave states, negro children to this very day are taught in separate schools while in the Northern States white and negro children attend the same schools."

In February 1913 Vladimir Ilyich wrote a special article entitled " Russians and Negroes," in which he strove to show that the ignorance, the cultural backwardness of one nationality affects the culture of other nationalities and that the cultural back-wardness of one class puts its stamp upon the culture of the entire country.

What Vladimir Ilyich said about proletarian policy in the sphere of education at that time is exceedingly interesting. In arguing against cultural autonomy, against "removing education from the sphere of control of the state," he wrote as follows: "The inter-ests of democracy in general and the interest of the working class in particular demand precisely the opposite. We must strive to secure that the children of all nationalities of a given locality attend the same school; that the workers of all nationalities *jointly* carry out the proletarian policy in education that was so well formulated by Samoilov, a delegate of the Vladimir workers, in the name of the Russian Social-Democratic Labour Party, in the Duma (Samoilov demanded the separation of the church from the state and the schools from the church; he demanded the complete secularisation of the schools)." Vladimir Ilyich also said that it would be easily possible to arrange for the children of the national minorities to study their own culture under real democracy when bureaucracy and Peredonov-ism* are driven from the schools.

In the summer of 1913 Ilyich wrote an outline of a speech Badayev was to deliver in the Duma on "The Policy of the Ministry of Education." In delivering this speech in the Duma, Badayev was continuously interrupted by the President of the Duma, and finally was prevented from finishing it. In this outline Ilyich quoted statistics showing the amazing cultural backwardness of the country and the insignificant sum assigned by the government for education. He showed how the policy of the tsarist government blocked the road to education for nine-tenths of the population. He described the government's treatment of teachers as "savage, shameful, disgusting and tyrannical." Here, too, he drew a comparison between Russia and America. In America, he wrote, 11 per cent. of the total population was illiterate but among the negroes 44 per cent. was illiterate; "nevertheless education is twice as high among American negroes as it is among the Russian peasants." Negroes were more literate than Russian peasants in 1900 because half a century before that

* Peredonov—a high-school teacher—character in Sologub's *Little Demon*, typifying the cringing, spiteful bureaucrat, servile to superiors and brutal to subordinates.

the American people defeated the American slave owners. The Russian people should also have overthrown their government in order to make their country a literate, cultured country.

Ilyich also wrote the outline of a speech for Comrade Shagov, in which he wrote that the only way by which Russia can become a literate country is by taking the land from the landowners and giving it to the peasants. In an article written at that time entitled "What can be Done for Education?" Ilyich described in great detail how libraries were organised in America and urged that the same system be adopted in Russia. In June he wrote an article entitled "The Working Class and Neo-Malthusianism," in which he wrote: "We are fighting better than our fathers did; our children will fight better than we are fighting and *they will be victorious*. The working class is not perishing, it is growing and becoming stronger, more manly, more united and is becoming enlightened and hardened in the struggle. We are pessimists in regard to feudalism, capitalism and small industry, but we are ardent optimists as far as the labour movement as a whole is concerned. We are laying the foundations for a new edifice and our children will complete it."

Ilyich gave his attention not only to questions of cultural development, but also to a number of other questions which have practical significance in socialist construction. Characteristic of this Cracow period are the articles he wrote like the one entitled "One of the Great Victories of Technique," in which he compared the rôle of great inventions under capitalism and under Socialism. Under capitalism, he wrote, inventions lead to the enrichment of a handful of millionaires, and to the worsening of the general conditions of life of the workers and to the growth of unemployment. "Under Socialism the application of Ramsay's method would release millions of miners from arduous toil and would immediately result in the shortening of the working day for all workers from eight hours to seven, for example, and even less. The electrification of all the factories and railways would make the conditions of labour much more hygienic and would relieve millions of workers from smoke, dust and dirt; the filthy, disgusting workshops would very soon be converted into clean and well lit laboratories worthy of human beings. Electric lighting and heating of all dwellings would relieve the millions of domestic slaves of the necessity of wasting three-fourths of their lives in dingy, smelly kitchens. Capitalist technique is every day more and more *outstripping* the social conditions, which condemn the toilers to complete slavery." Seventeen years ago Ilyich was already thinking about "electrification, a seven-hour day, about factory kitchens and the emancipation of women."

The article entitled "A Fashionable Branch of Industry," showed that seventeen years ago Ilyich was already thinking about the significance of the automobile industry under socialism. In his article "Iron in Agriculture," Ilyich describes iron as the "foundation of the culture of a country." "We all like to talk a great deal about culture, about the development of productive forces, about raising peasant economy to a higher level, etc.," he wrote, "but as soon as the question arises of removing the obstacle which stands in the way of 'raising' the millions of poverty-stricken, down-trodden, hungry, barefooted, uncivilised peasants to a higher level, then our millionaires lose their power of speech . . . our industrial magnates prefer to share

their mediaeval privileges with the Purishkeviches*
and to sigh about the liberation of the 'fatherland'
from mediaeval lack of culture."

But Ilyich's article, "The Ideas of Progressive
Capital," is particularly interesting. In this article
he discusses the ideas of an American millionaire
business man named Filene, who tried to persuade
the masses to accept the employers as their leaders,
because the employers were learning more and more
to understand their interests and because the interests of the employers and the masses were common
interests. Democracy is developing, Ilyich wrote in
this article, the strength of the masses is growing, the
cost of living is rising. Parliament and the daily
Press with its huge circulations are making the
masses more and more informed. Hence the aim of
the progressive capitalists is to fool the masses, to
make them believe that there is no antagonism of
interests between labour and capital and they are
prepared to spend a certain amount of money (by
giving office employees and skilled workers a share
in the profits) in order to achieve their aim. After
examining the ideas of progressive capitalism, Ilyich
exclaims: "Most esteemed Mr. Filene! are you fully
convinced that the workers of the whole world are
such fools?"

These articles, written seventeen years ago, show
how much interested Ilyich was in problems of
construction at that time. When the Soviet government was established these problems were already
familiar to him; all that had to be done was to apply
the solutions that he had already worked out.

* Purishkevich, a Bessarabian landlord and diehard reactionary;
founder of the notorious League of Russian People better known as
the "Black Hundred," which, aided and abetted by the tsarist police,
perpetrated the progroms or murderous mob attacks on Jews and
revolutionaries.—Ed.

In the autumn of 1912 we made the acquaintance of Nikolai Ivanovich Bukharin. Besides Bagotsky, whom we frequently met, Casimir Chapinski, a Pole who worked on the Cracow newspaper *Napshud* (*Forward*), visited us. He told us a great deal about the famous Cracow resort Zakopane and described the glorious mountains and beauty of the place. Incidentally, he told us that a Social-Democrat named Orlov, who was making beautiful paintings of the Zakopane mountains, was living there. One day, soon after we had moved from Zvezhintsa to the city, we were looking through the window and observed a youngish-looking man, carrying a large canvas bag on his back, coming towards the house. This proved to be Orlov—otherwise Bukharin. He and Ilyich had quite a long talk that day. Bukharin lived in Vienna. From that time onwards close connection was established with Vienna. The Troyanovskys lived there, too. When we asked Nikolai Ivanovich (Bukharin) about his paintings he took a number of splendid paintings by German artists from his bag and we examined them with great interest. Among them were works by Beckling and a number of other artists. Vladimir Ilyich liked pictures very much. I remember how surprised I was when one evening when we visited Vorovsky, Ilyich found a heap of illustrated descriptions of the works of various artists and read them and studied the reproductions of the pictures with great interest throughout the evening.

Many people visited us at Cracow at that time. Comrades who were on their way to Russia would stop to make arrangements about their work. One day Nikolai Nikolaevich Yakovlev, the brother of Varvara Nikolaevna, came to visit us and stayed for about two weeks. He was on his way to Moscow, where he was to start a Bolshevik paper *Nash Put* (*Our Way*). He was a staunch and reliable Bolshevik. Ilyich had long talks with him. Yakovlev started the paper, but it was soon suppressed and he was arrested. This is not surprising for Malinovsky,* the Moscow delegate, "helped" to start the paper. When he was with us Malinovsky told us a great deal about the journeys he had made through the Moscow province and about the workers' meetings which he said he had conducted. Once he told us about a meeting at which he said a policeman was present who listened very attentively and tried to be helpful. While relating this incident Malinovsky laughed. Generally he liked to talk a great deal about himself. He told us why he had volunteered for the Russo-Japanese war. He was at a recruiting office, he said, to report in answer to the mobilisation order when a demonstration passed by. He could not control himself, and he made a speech from the window. He was arrested for this and the colonel came to him and said he would not send him to a military prison if he volunteered to go to war. He had no alternative but to go, said Malinovsky. He also told us that his wife was religious and that when she discovered that he was an atheist she tried to commit suicide, and that she frequently had nervous fits after that. Malinovsky's tales seemed queer to us. No doubt there was some truth in them. He told us what he had actually experienced, but he did not tell us the whole truth; he left out the most important points and many pictures he painted in false colours. Later on I thought—perhaps the story he told us about what happened at the recruiting office was true and that perhaps on returning from the war the police presented him with an ultimatum either to become an

* Later proved to be an *agent provocateur*—Ed.

agent provocateur or to go to prison. Perhaps his wife was of a morbid nature, and did really attempt to commit suicide, but the reason may have been some other than that which Malinovsky gave us; perhaps she suspected her husband of being an *agent provocateur*. At all events Malinovsky's tales were interwoven with truth and this made them sound plausible. It did not occur to anyone at the time that he was a police spy.

The government tried to place another *agent provocateur* on the *Pravda* in addition to Malinovsky. This was Chernomazov. He lived in Paris and on his way to Russia he, too, stopped at Cracow and brought us a letter from Piatnitsky. He was going to work for *Pravda*. We did not like Chernomazov and I did not even ask him to stay the night with us, so he was compelled to spend the night walking the streets of Cracow.

Ilyich attached tremendous importance to *Pravda* and wrote articles almost every day for it. He would carefully note where collections had been made for the paper, how much had been collected, how many articles were written for it, on what subjects, etc. He was exceedingly happy when the paper published good articles and pursued a correct policy. Once, at the end of 1913, he asked *Pravda* to send him a list of its subscribers and for about two weeks my mother and I sat evening after evening sorting the names of the subscribers according to the cities in which they lived. Nine-tenths of the subscribers were workers. We would come across a town with many subscribers. On looking up the town we found that there was a large factory there about which we had not known. The chart which we drew up showing the distribution of the *Pravda* was a very interesting one; Ilyich was very pleased with it, but it was never printed. In all probability Chernomazov threw it into the waste-paper basket. But much worse things than this happened. Sometimes, although rarely, Ilyich's articles would get lost. Sometimes his articles would be held up and printed only after some delay. This irritated Ilyich and he wrote angry letters to *Pravda*, but that did not improve matters.

We were not only visited by comrades passing through Cracow on the way to Russia, but also by those coming from Russia who would call in to get advice about various matters. I remember when Nikolai Vassilievich Krylenko arrived soon after Inessa had visited him. He came in order to make more definite arrangements about connections. I remember how glad Ilyich was when he arrived. In the summer of 1913 Gnevich and Dansky arrived in order to make arrangements for publishing the magazine *Insurance Questions*, which was to be published by the Priboy Publishing Company. This was in connection with the forthcoming elections of the insurance funds committees in Russia. Ilyich attached great importance to this election and believed that the election campaign would strengthen our contacts with the masses.

In the middle of February 1913 a conference of the members of the Central Committee was held in Cracow. Our Duma deputies arrived. Stalin also arrived. Ilyich had met Stalin at the Tammerfors Conference and at the Stockholm and London Congresses. Ilyich had long discussions with Stalin on the national question. He was glad to meet a man who was seriously interested in this question and who was well informed on it. Prior to his arrival in Cracow Stalin had spent two months in Vienna where he had studied the national question. There he became closely connected with our people,

Bukharin and Troyanovsky. After the conference
Ilyich wrote to Gorky about Stalin as follows: "We
have a wonderful Georgian here who is writing a
long article for *Prosveshchenie*. He has collected all the
Austrian as well as other material for it." At that time
Ilyich was worried about the *Pravda*, and so also was
Stalin. They discussed methods for putting things
right. I think Comrade Troyanovsky was invited to
these discussions. Vladimir Ilyich had great faith
in the Troyanovskys and expected a great deal of
them. Elena Fedorovna Troyanovskaya (Rozmirovich), was preparing to go to Russia. At this conference the position of *Prosveshchenie* was discussed and
also the question of *Pravda* issuing a series of pamphlets. Wide plans were drawn up.

Just before this a parcel arrived from home containing salmon, caviar and sturgeon. I borrowed a
cookery book from my mother and gave a party.
Vladimir Ilyich, who loved to treat his comrades to the
best he had, was highly satisfied with the whole affair.

On his return to Russia Stalin was arrested in St.
Petersburg on February 22nd.

Our life in Cracow was rather monotonous when
there were no visitors. "We are living here as if we
were in Shushya,"* I wrote to Ilyich's mother, "the
coming of the postman is the greatest event to look
forward to. Until eleven o'clock we try to pass the
time away somehow or another. At eleven o'clock
the postman comes and then he comes again at six—
we can hardly wait so long." Vladimir Ilyich did
not like the Cracow libraries much. He tried skating
on the ice, but spring soon came. At Easter time
we took a trip to the Volsky forest. Spring is beautiful in Cracow and in the forest it was simply glorious.

* The Siberian village where Lenin and Krupshaya spent their
exile.—Ed.

The bushes blossomed forth in yellow bloom and the sap was rising in the branches of the trees. One could feel the spring all around. Spring is intoxicating. It took us quite a while to get back to town, however, and in order to reach home we had to cross the entire city on foot. The trams were not running owing to the Easter holidays. I was quite exhausted when we got home. I had been rather ill during the winter of 1913. Something went wrong with my heart; my hands trembled and I suffered from general weakness. Ilyich insisted on my going to see a doctor. The doctor said my case was serious, that my nerves were overstrained and my heart was weak. He advised me to go to the mountains in Zakopane. When I came home I related what the doctor had said. The cobbler's wife, who came to see to the stove and did our shopping, waxed indignant: "Who said you are nervous—big ladies are nervous and throw the dishes about!" I did not throw dishes about, but in the state I was in I was not fit for work.

We decided to move to Poronin, seven kilometres from Zakopane, for the summer. Zakopane was too overcrowded and expensive; Poronin was simpler and less expensive. We, that is, the Zinovievs, the Bagotskys and their famous dog Zhulik, rented a large bungalow and moved out together. This bungalow was situated 700 metres above sea-level at the foot of the Tatra mountains. The air was wonderful, and although there were frequent mists and drizzle the view of the mountains during the clear intervals was extremely beautiful. We would climb up to the plateau which was quite close to our bungalow and watch the snow-capped peaks of the Tatra mountains; they were beautiful. Sometimes Ilyich and Bagotsky would go to Zakopane to visit Vigelev and take long walks in the mountains with him. Ilyich was exceedingly fond of walking. The mountain air helped me very little. My health got worse and after consulting Bagotsky, who was a neurologist, Ilyich insisted on me going to Berne to be operated on by Kocher. We went there in the middle of June. On our way we stopped in Vienna and visited the Bukharins. Nadezhda Mikhailovna, Bukharin's wife, was very sick and Bukharin had to look after the house. Putting sugar instead of salt into the soup, he talked animatedly with Ilyich about questions which interested Ilyich and about our people who lived in Vienna. We met some of the Vienna comrades and rode about the town with them. Vienna has a charm of its own. It is a large capital city and in contrast with Cracow we were greatly impressed by it. In Berne the Shklovskys took charge of us and fussed over us a great deal. They lived in a little detached cottage with a garden. Ilyich joked with the younger girls and teased Jenurka. I stayed in the hospital about three weeks. Ilyich would stay with me half the day and spend the rest of the day in the libraries. He read a great deal; he even read a number of medical books on my disease and took extensive notes on questions that interested him. While I was in the hospital he visited Zurich, Geneva and Lausanne to deliver lectures on the national question. He also lectured on the subject in Berne. In Berne,—this was after I left the hospital—a conference of the groups abroad was held at which the state of Party affairs was discussed. After the operation I had to spend about two weeks recuperating in the mountains in Guttenberg, where Kocher advised me to go, but we received word from Poronin that there were many urgent affairs to be settled and on the receipt of a telegram from Zinoviev we went back.

On the way we stopped at Munich. Boris Knipovich, a nephew of Lydia Mikhailovna Knipovich
(known as Dyadenka), lived there. I had known him
since he was quite a child when I used to tell him
fairy tales. He—the four-year-old blue-eyed little
Boris—would climb up on my knees, put his arms
round my neck and say: "Krupa, tell me the story
about the little tin Soldier." In 1905-07 Boris was
an active organiser of Social-Democratic groups
among college students. In the summer of 1907, after
the London Congress, Ilyich had lived with the
Knipoviches in the village of Stirsudden in Finland.
At that time Boris was still a college student, but he
was already interested in Marxism and would listen
with rapt attention to what Ilyich had to say. He
revered and loved both Ilyich and Dyadenka. In
1911 he was arrested and later was exiled abroad.
He went to Munich and studied at the Munich
University. In 1912 he published his first book on
The Differentiation Among the Russian Peasantry, a copy
of which he sent to Ilyich. In reply Ilyich wrote him
a letter in which he displayed particular attention
and interest in the young author. "I read your book
with great pleasure," he wrote, "and I was very glad
that you undertook to write a big and serious work.
A work of this kind will certainly enable you to test,
deepen and strengthen your Marxian convictions."
And then Lenin proceeded very discreetly to suggest
several corrections and give him advice as to method.

On re-reading this letter, I recall Ilyich's attitude
towards inexperienced authors. In discussing their
work with them he would get right down to the heart
of the subject, to the fundamentals and make suggestions for improvement. But he did all this very
discreetly, so that these authors hardly noticed that
they were being corrected. And Ilyich was very

I

good at helping people in their work. If, for example, he wanted someone to write an article but was not sure whether he would be able to do it properly, he would start a discussion with him, expound his ideas and get the prospective writer interested. After he had sounded him on the subject sufficiently, he would say to him: "Would you like to write an article on this subject?" And the author would not even have noticed that his preliminary discussion with Ilyich had helped him and that in writing his article he had actually used Ilyich's expressions and turns of phrase.

We would have liked to stay at Munich for several days to see the changes that had taken place since the time we lived there in 1902, but we were in such a hurry to get back that we stayed there only for several hours until we got the train. Boris and his wife came to meet us. We spent the time in the restaurant which was famous for its Hof-brau beer. On the walls and on the beer-mugs were inscribed the initials H. B., which looked like the Russian letters N. V. "This is the Narodnaya Volya beer-house," I said in jest. Ilyich praised the Munich beer as if he were a connoisseur. He and Boris talked about the class differentiation among the peasantry, and his wife and I talked about Dyadenka who just then was very sick. Ilyich jotted down a few lines to her, urging her to go abroad and be operated upon by Kocher. We arrived at Poronin at the beginning of August—I think it was the sixth. There we were met by the usual Poronin rain, by Lev Borisovich Kamenev and a great deal of news about Russia.

A conference of the members of the Central Committee had been arranged for the 9th. *Pravda* had been closed down. In its place *Rabochaya Pravda*

(*Workers' Truth*) was being published, but almost
every number was suppressed. Strikes were breaking
out everywhere—in St. Petersburg, Riga, Nikolayev
and Baku. Of the Duma deputies present I remember only Malinovsky. The conference discussed the
affairs of *Rabochaya Pravda*, the Moscow *Prosveshchenie* and the Priboy Publishing House, the tactics to
be pursued at the forthcoming co-operative and com-
mercial class congresses and other urgent problems.

Kamenev moved into the flat above ours, and in
the evenings he and Ilyich, after dinner, would stay
in our large kitchen and discuss the news from Russia.

Preparations were going forward for the Party
Conference, which became known as the "summer
conference." This was held in Poronin from September 21st to October 1st. All the Duma deputies
arrived except Samoilov. There were also two
Moscow electors, Novozhilov and Balashov, Rozmirovich from Kiev, Sima Deryabina from the Urals,
Shotman from St. Petersburg and others. *Prosveshchenie* was represented by Troyanovsky, the
Poles by Ganetsky, Domsky and by two Rozlamovists (the influence of the Rozlamovists at that time
had spread over the four largest industrial districts
in Poland—Warsaw, Lodz, Dombrow and Kalish).
While the conference was in progress Inessa arrived.
She was arrested in September 1912 with a false
passport. Conditions in prison were very hard and
had undermined her health; she showed symptoms
of tuberculosis, but she had not lost any of her energy
and flung herself into Party work with all her usual
ardour. We were all very glad that she had arrived.
In all there were twenty-four persons present at the
conference.

At the conference it was decided to raise the question of convening a Party congress. Six years had

passed since the Fifth Congress held in London and there had been many changes since then. The questions before the conference were as follows: the strike movement, the preparations for the general political strike, the tasks of agitation, the publication of a number of popular pamphlets, the inadmissability of modifying the slogans—Democratic Republic, Confiscation of the Landlords' Land and the Eight-Hour Day in the course of carrying on agitation. The question of how to carry on work in legal societies and how to carry on Social-Democratic work in the Duma was discussed. The decisions on the necessity of obtaining equal rights for the Bolsheviks in the Social-Democratic Duma fraction and on preventing the Bolsheviks in the fraction from being voted down by a majority of one, by the "seven"* who represented only an insignificant minority of the workers, were particularly important. The other important resolution which was passed was that on the national question which expressed the views of Vladimir Ilyich. I remember the disputes which took place in our kitchen on this question. I remember the passions that were roused around it and the ardour with which it was discussed.

This time Malinovsky was in a terribly nervous state; he would get drunk night after night, would become maudlin and complain that he was mistrusted. The Moscow electors, Balashov and Novozhilov, were very indignant at his behaviour. They sensed a certain falseness and play-acting in Malinovsky's stories and conduct.

* As has been previously explained, the Social-Democratic deputies in the Duma numbered thirteen, six Bolsheviks and seven Mensheviks, although the Bolsheviks represented a far larger number of workers than the Mensheviks. The Mensheviks, however, took advantage of their majority of one to force their line of policy on the whole of the Duma fraction.

We remained in Poronin for another two weeks after the conference. We walked a great deal and visited Cherny Stav, a mountain lake of extraordinary beauty, and other places in the mountains.

All of us, the entire Cracow group, became very much attached to Inessa. She always seemed to be in good spirits and full of vigour. We had known her in Paris, but there was a large colony there, whereas in Cracow we lived in a small, comradely, isolated circle. Inessa rented a room in the same flat where Kamenev lived. My mother grew very fond of her and often visited her to have a chat and a smoke. It seemed cosier and livelier when Inessa was present.

We were all absorbed in Party affairs and our mode of life resembled that of students rather than family life and we were very glad to have Inessa. She told us a great deal about her life and about her children; she showed me their letters and in speaking about them she seemed to radiate warmth and ardour. Ilyich, Inessa and myself did a lot of walking. Zinoviev and Kamenev dubbed us the "Hikers' Party." We usually took walks along the meadows outside the city. The Polish word for meadow is *blon*, and it was from that that Inessa assumed the pseudonym of Blonina. Inessa loved music and made us attend Beethoven concerts. She herself was a good musician and played many of Beethoven's compositions very well indeed. Ilyich was particularly fond of the *Sonate Pathétique* and he always asked her to play it. Ilyich, too, loved music. Later, in Soviet times now, he would visit Comrade Tsurupa to hear the Sonata played by some famous musician. We talked a lot about fiction. "The thing we are starved for here is fiction," I wrote to Ilyich's mother. "Volodya* has nearly learnt the works of Nadson

* The pet name for Vladimir.—Ed.

and Nekrasov by heart and the only volume we
possess of *Anna Karenina* has been read and re-read
for the hundredth time. We left our works of fiction,
an insignificant part of what we had in St. Petersburg, in Paris and here we cannot get any Russian
books. Sometimes we greedily read the advertisements of second-hand book dealers advertising
twenty-eight volumes of Uspensky, ten volumes of
Pushkin, etc., etc. To make matters worse, Volodya
has suddenly become a great lover of *belles-lettres*.
And he is a terrible nationalist. He would not go to
see the works of Polish painters for anything. But
one day he picked up a catalogue of the Tretyakov
Galleries at the home of one of our friends and frequently becomes absorbed in it."

At first we thought that Inessa would remain in
Cracow and would bring her children over from
Russia. I even helped her to look for an apartment.
But we lived a very isolated life in Cracow which
reminded one somewhat of exile. There was nothing
in Cracow which could provide Inessa with an out-
let for her abundant energies. She decided to make
the rounds of our groups abroad and deliver a series
of lectures and then to settle in Paris in order to
organise the work of our committee abroad. Before
her departure I had long talks with her about women's work. She strongly insisted upon the necessity
for conducting propaganda work among women
workers, and of publishing a special women workers'
magazine in St. Petersburg. Ilyich wrote to Anna
Ilyinishna about the publication of such a magazine
which was published soon after. Later on Inessa did
a great deal for the development of work among
working women and devoted much effort to this.

In January 1914 Malinovsky came to Cracow and
he and Ilyich went to Paris and from there to

Brussels to attend the Fourth Congress of the Lettish Social-Democrats which was opened on January 13th.

In Paris Malinovsky delivered what in Ilyich's opinion was a very able report on the work of the Duma fraction and Ilyich delivered a lengthy address on the national question. He also spoke at a meeting in memory of January 9th.* In addition he spoke at a meeting of the Bolshevik group in Paris on the intervention of the International Socialist Bureau in Russian Affairs and on the statement that Kautsky made at the December meeting of the International Socialist Bureau to the effect that the Social-Democratic Party in Russia was dead. Ilyich was greatly disturbed by the decision of the International Socialist Bureau to intervene in Russian affairs, because he thought that that would merely serve to retard the growing influence of the Bolsheviks in Russia. Ilyich sent a report to Huysmans, the Secretary of the International Bureau, on the situation in the Party. The Fourth Congress of the Lettish Social-Democrats resulted in a victory for the Bolsheviks. At this congress Comrades Berzin, Latsis, Herman and a number of other Lettish Bolsheviks were present. Ilyich spoke at the Congress and appealed to the Letts to affiliate to the Central Committee. In a letter to his mother Ilyich wrote that the trip to Paris had refreshed him. " Paris is not a city for people with modest means; it is very tiring," he wrote. "But for a short visit there is not a better or livelier city. It braced me up very much."

In the winter, soon after Vladimir Ilyich returned from Paris, it was decided that Kamenev should go

* I.e. Bloody Sunday, 1905, when the tsarist troops shot down the workers, who had peacefully come to present a petition to him at the Winter Palace in St. Petersburg.—Ed.

to Russia to take charge of *Pravda* and to supervise the work of the Duma fraction. Both the newspaper and the Duma fraction needed help. In the meantime Kamenev's wife and little son arrived. Kamenev's little son and little Stepa Zinoviev had heated discussions as to whether St. Petersburg was a city or Russia. The departure for Russia began. We all went to the station to see them off. It was a cold winter evening. We spoke very little. Only Kamenev's little son kept up a steady chatter. Everyone was wrapped up in his own thoughts. We all asked ourselves how long Kamenev would hold out, how soon would we meet? When would we be able to go to Russia? Each of us secretly thought about Russia; each of us had a strong desire to go. Night after night I would dream about Nevaskaya Zastava (a suburb of St. Petersburg). We avoided speaking of this subject but all of us secretly thought about it.

On March 8th, 1914, International Women's Day, the first number of the popular magazine *Rabotnitza* (*The Woman Worker*) appeared in St. Petersburg. It was sold at four kopeks a copy. The St. Petersburg Party committee issued leaflets on Women's Day. Inessa and Stahl wrote articles for the magazine from Paris and Lilina and I wrote from Cracow. Seven numbers of this magazine were published. We were preparing No. 8 and planned to have articles on the Socialist Women's Congress which was to take place in Vienna, but that issue never appeared—the war broke out.

We tried to convene a Party Congress to take place at the same time as the International Socialist Congress which was to take place in Vienna in August. We hoped that some of the delegates would be able to come legally. Then it was planned that the crossing of the border *en masse* should be organised under the guise of an excursion. This was to be arranged by the printers in Cracow.

In May we moved back again to Poronin.

In order to prepare the campaign for the congress in St. Petersburg, Comrades Kisilev, Glebov-Avilov and Anna Nikiforova were mobilised. They came to Poronin to discuss the arrangements with Ilyich. On the first day of their arrival we sat for a long time on top of a little hill near our bungalow and they told us about the work in Russia. They were all young, full of energy and made a good impression upon Ilyich. Glebov-Avilov kept exchanging glances with Kisilev. The following day they told us the reason for this. Glebov-Avilov had been a pupil at the Bologna school, but had now left the *Vperyod*-ists. Ilyich advised the visitors to take a walk in the mountains. He was not feeling very well himself, so they went without him. When they returned, they laughingly told us where they had been. They had climbed up a very steep peak, they said, and their knapsacks kept getting in their way, so they took turns in carrying them. When it was Anna's turn all the passers-by chaffed her, and ironically advised her to put her friends on her shoulders as well.

Finally, the character of the agitation to be carried on at the congress was decided upon. Having received all the necessary instructions Kisilev went to the Baltic region and Glebov-Avilov and Anna went to the Ukraine.

Among those who came from Moscow was Alya, a former Capri student, who, it later turned out, was an *agent provocateur*. I cannot recall on what pretext he came, but he wanted information about the congress which was to be held shortly. The secret police, of course, wanted to have more authentic information about the congress and so they sent him.

Inessa brought her children over from Russia for the summer and lived in Trieste by the sea. She was preparing a report on the International Women's Congress which was to be held in Vienna at the same time as the International Socialist Congress. She also had work to do in other fields. In the middle of June the International Socialist Bureau decided to call a conference in Brussels of representatives of eleven organisations of the Russian Social-Democratic Labour Party representing all shades of opinion in order to discuss the differences that prevailed and to establish unity. It was clear, however, that the conference would not be confined to this question and that the liquidators, the Trotskyists, the Bundists and others would take advantage of the occasion in order to try to restrict the activities of the Bolsheviks and to bind them by a number of decisions. In Russia the influence of the Bolsheviks was growing. As Comrade Badayev points out in his book, *The Bolsheviks in the Tsarist Duma*, in the summer of 1914 the Bolsheviks had the majority on the executive committees of fourteen out of the eighteen trade unions in St. Petersburg. The stronger unions, including the Metal Workers' Union which was the largest and strongest union in St. Petersburg, was on the side of the Bolsheviks. The same thing was evident among the workers' groups in the insurance organisations. Of the Insurance Fund delegates elected in St. Petersburg and Moscow, thirty-seven were Bolsheviks and only seven were Mensheviks, and of the delegates elected to the All-Russian Insurance Fund Committee, forty-seven were Bolsheviks and ten were Mensheviks. The election of delegates to the International Congress in Vienna was well organised. The majority of the workers' organisations elected Bolsheviks.

The preparations for the Party Congress were also proceeding successfully. " The task that confronted us," writes Badayev in his book, "namely, to strengthen and widen the local Party cells before the congress, was fulfilled to a large extent, thanks to the tremendous upsurge that had taken place in the revolutionary movement in the country during the past few months. The workers' swing towards the Party increased; new cadres of revolutionary-minded workers joined the Party organisation. The work of leading the Party groups was constantly improving. Thanks to this the forthcoming congress and the questions on its agenda were assured of the close attention of the Party masses."*

Badayev collected considerable sums of money for the fund for organising the congress. He had already received a number of mandates and resolutions on questions to be raised at the congress, instructions to delegates, etc. He vividly describes how all the illegal work was interwoven with legal activities. He writes as follows:

" Summer presented us with an opportunity of organising illegal meetings outside of the city, in the woods, where we were comparatively safe from police raids. When it was necessary to call more or less general meetings they were arranged under the guise of excursions to the country in the name of some educational society. After leaving St. Petersburg a couple of dozen versts behind we would go 'for a walk' into the depth of the forest. We would then place patrols who would direct the way only by a previously arranged password and then we would hold our meeting. . . . Spies, in great numbers, surrounded all the labour organisations, paying particular attention to well-known centres which

* A. E. Badayev, *The Bolsheviks in the Tsarist Duma*, p. 189.

carried on Party work, such as the editorial office of the *Pravda* and the rooms where our fraction met. But while the activity of the secret police increased we managed to improve our technique of secrecy. There were, of course, arrests of single comrades but no general arrests occurred."*

Thus, the line followed by the Central Committee to develop the issue of legal publications, to give them a definite direction, to develop the work of the Duma fraction inside and outside of the Duma, to present all questions clearly and distinctly and to combine legal with illegal work, proved to be absolutely correct.

The attempt on the part of the International Socialist Bureau to prevent this line from being pursued and to hinder this work enraged Ilyich. He decided not to go to the Brussels Unity Conference. Inessa was to go. She spoke French (like a native), never got confused and had a strong will. She could be depended upon not to surrender the position. Inessa lived in Trieste and Ilyich sent her a report of the Central Committee which he had drawn up and a number of instructions as to how she was to act in particular circumstances. He thought of and provided for all contingencies. In addition to Inessa the delegation of the Central Committee consisted of M. F. Vladimirsky and N. F. Popov. Inessa was to submit the report of the Central Committee in French. As was to be expected, matters were not limited merely to an exchange of opinion at the conference. Kautsky, in the name of the Bureau, submitted a resolution disapproving of the split and declaring that there were no important differences of opinion between the various fractions. All voted for the resolution except the delegates of the Central

* A. E. Badayev, *The Bolsheviks in the Tsarist Duma*, p. 190.

Committee and the Lettish comrades who refused to vote in spite of Huysmans' threat that he would report to the Vienna Congress, that those who did not vote must be held responsible for disrupting the attempt to bring about unity.

At a private conference in Brussels the liquidators, the Trotskyists, the *Vperyod*-ists, the Plekhanovists and the Caucasian District Organisation formed a *bloc* against the Bolsheviks. This *bloc* decided to take advantage of the situation which had arisen in order to bring pressure on the Bolsheviks.

Besides the Brussels unity business, Ilyich's attention in the summer of 1914 was concentrated on another very serious affair, i.e. the Malinovsky affair.

General Junkovsky was appointed Vice Minister of the Interior and he discovered that Malinovsky was in the employ of the secret police. He reported this to Rodzyanko, the President of the Duma, and pointed out to him that as Malinovsky was a member of the Duma this would lead to a grave political scandal if it became publicly known. On May 8th Malinovsky handed in his resignation from the Duma to Rodzyanko and informed the members of the Social-Democratic fraction of this. The reason he gave for his resignation was "private affairs," but he did not say what these affairs were. After resigning he went abroad. The local and central Party organisations condemned Malinovsky's action as anarchistic and disruptive and expelled him from the Party. The charge that Malinovsky was a *provocateur* seemed so monstrous that the Central Committee appointed a special commission under the chairmanship of Donetsky, and included Lenin and Zinoviev, to inquire into it. Rumours about Malinovsky being an *agent provocateur* had been circulating for a long time. These rumours came from Menshevik circles. Elena Fedorovna Rozmirovich had strong suspicions in connection with her arrest—she had worked with the Duma fraction. The gendarmes who questioned her possessed information about details which they could have obtained only from spies inside the organisation. Bukharin also had certain information about Malinovsky's conduct. Vladimir Ilyich thought it utterly impossible for Malinovsky to have been an *agent provocateur*. Only once did a doubt flash across his mind. I remember one day in Poronin, we were returning from the Zinovievs and talked about these rumours. Suddenly Ilyich stopped on the little bridge that we were crossing and said: "It may be true!" and his face expressed anxiety. "What are you talking about, it's nonsense." I answered deprecatingly. Ilyich calmed down and began to abuse the Mensheviks, saying that they were unscrupulous as to the means they employed in the struggle against the Bolsheviks. He had no other doubts on this question.

The commission investigated all the rumours about Malinovsky; they heard Burtzev's opinion that the accusation was improbable and questioned Bukharin and Rozmirovich; but they could not obtain any definite proof of the charge.

Completely knocked out of action and in a state of suspense Malinovsky idled about Poronin. Allah knows what he lived through during this time. Then he disappeared, nobody knew where. His true character was definitely revealed after the February Revolution. After the October Revolution he voluntarily returned to Russia, gave himself up to the Soviet government and was tried and sentenced to death by the Supreme Revolutionary Tribunal.

Meanwhile the struggle in Russia became more acute. The strike movement was spreading, particularly in Baku. The masses of the workers supported the Baku strikers. In St. Petersburg the police shot into a crowd of 12,000 Putilov workers. Conflicts with the police were becoming more fierce. The Duma deputies were becoming leaders of the rising proletariat. Mass strikes became the order of the day. On July 7th, 130,000 workers came out on strike in St. Petersburg. The proletariat was preparing for battle. The strikes did not subside; on the contrary they grew in intensity. Barricades were thrown up on the streets of red St. Petersburg.

Then the war broke out.

On August 1st Germany declared war on Russia. On August 3rd she declared war on France; on August 4th she declared war on Belgium and on that very day England declared war on her. On August 6th Austria declared war on Russia; on August 11th France and England declared war on Austria.

The world war started and for a time checked the growing revolutionary movement in Russia. It upset the whole world. It gave rise to a number of profound crises; it raised the most important problems of the revolutionary struggle in a new and sharper form; it brought out the whole of the proletariat as the leader of all the toilers; it roused new sections of society to the struggle; it made the victory of the proletariat a question of life or death for Russia.

THE YEARS OF THE WAR TO THE FEBRU-
ARY REVOLUTION (1914-17)

CRACOW (1914)

ALTHOUGH war had long been in the air, when it was actually declared it came as a shock to all. We had to leave Poronin, but had as yet no idea where to go. Lilina was very ill at the time, and Zinoviev could not leave anyhow. At that time they lived in Zakopane where physicians were available. We therefore decided to stay for the time being in Poronin. Ilyich wrote to Kobetzky at Copenhagen asking to be kept informed, to establish connections with Stockholm, etc. The local mountain population was utterly depressed when mobilisation began. No one had any clear idea whom the war was against and why it was being fought; there was no enthusiasm, and men went as if led to slaughter. Our hostess, the owner of the cottage, a peasant woman, was crushed with grief; her husband was drafted for the war. From the pulpit the Catholic priest tried to rouse patriotic sentiments. All sorts of rumours began to spread, and the six-year-old boy of a neighbouring poor family who had been hanging around our house, informed me with an air of mystery that the Russians—so the priest said—were putting poison into the wells.

On August 7th the quartermaster of the local *gendarmes* came to our house accompanied by a witness, a local peasant armed with a rifle, to make a search. The officer did not quite know what he was to search for, fumbled in the book-case, found an unloaded Browning pistol, took several notebooks containing statistics on the agrarian problem and asked a few insignificant questions. The witness, in a state of embarrassment, sat on the edge of a chair and looked about in a perplexed manner. The *gendarme* officer poked fun at him and, pointing to a jar of paste, said it was a bomb. Then the officer said that there was a formal complaint against Vladimir Ilyich, and that he really should arrest him, but since he would have to deliver the prisoner to-morrow morning to Novy Targ, the nearest town where military authorities were stationed, it would be just as well for Ilyich to report in the morning in time to board the six o'clock train. The danger of arrest was obvious, and in war time, during the first days of the war, they could easily put him out of the way. Vladimir Ilyich went to see Ganetsky, who also lived in Poronin, and told him of what had taken place. Ganetsky immediately telegraphed to the Social-Democratic deputy Mareck, and Vladimir Ilyich telegraphed to the police in Cracow, where he was known as a political exile. Ilyich was worried how mother and I would stay alone in the big house in Poronin. He arranged with Comrade Tichomirnov that the latter live with us in the upper room. Tichomirnov had returned recently from exile in Olonetsk, and the editorial committee of *Pravda* sent him to Poronin to regain his health which had been shattered during his exile, also incidentally to help Ilyich prepare data in connection with the current campaigns for the labour press, etc.—on the basis of material printed in *Pravda*.

Ilyich and I stayed up all night. We could not sleep, the situation was so alarming. In the morning I saw him off and came back to an empty room. On

K

the same day, Ganetsky hired a cart to take him to
Novy Targ. There he succeeded in seeing the regional
commander; he made a great fuss, told the commander that Ilyich was a member of the International Socialist Bureau, a man for whom many
would intercede and for whose life he, the commander, would have to answer. He also saw the
public prosecutor, told him who Ilyich was, and
obtained permission for me to see him on the very
next day. When Ganetsky returned from Novy
Targ we both composed a letter to Vienna to Victor
Adler, member of the International Bureau and
Social-Democratic deputy in the Austrian Parliament. At Novy Targ I was permitted to see Ilyich.
We were left alone, but Ilyich spoke little—the
situation was still quite confused. The police of
Cracow telegraphed that there were no grounds for
suspecting Ulyanov of espionage. A similar telegram
was sent by Mareck from Zakopane, and a well-
known Polish writer came to Novy Targ to intercede
on behalf of Ilyich. When he heard of Ilyich's arrest,
Zinoviev, who lived in Zakopane, despite the pour-
ing rain, cycled to see the old member of the Narodnaya Volya Party, the Polish Dr. Dlussky, who lived
ten miles from Zakopane. Dlussky immediately
hired a carriage and went to Zakopane, where he
did considerable telegraphing and letter-writing and
then went somewhere to conduct negotiations. I was
permitted to visit Ilyich daily. Early in the morning
I would leave on the six o'clock train for Novy Targ,
an hour's ride, then until eleven o'clock I would
wander about the station, the post office and the
market-place, and then have an hour's interview
with Vladimir Ilyich. Ilyich spoke to me about his
prison mates. There were many local peasants in
the prison—some for carrying passports whose legal

date had expired, others for non-payment of taxes, and others because they had fallen foul of the local authorities. Among the prisoners there was a Frenchman, a Polish petty official who travelled on someone else's reduced rate ticket for the sake of economy, a gypsy who called to his wife from the prison-yard across the wall where the woman would come at a set hour. Ilyich recalled that when he was in exile in Shushenskoye he used to give legal advice to the local peasants whom he got out of all kinds of difficulties, and in the prison he set up an improvised legal advice bureau, writing petitions, etc. His prison mates nicknamed Ilyich "Bitchiy Khlop," meaning "sturdy peasant." "Bitchiy Khlop" became acclimatised to the prison at Novy Targ and was more alert and calm at our meetings. In this criminal prison, at night when the inmates were asleep, he made plans for the further course of the Party, the measures that would have to be taken in order to turn the world war into a world conflict between the proletariat and the bourgeoisie. I told Ilyich the news of the war that I had succeeded in obtaining.

I did not tell him the following: once while returning from the railway station I heard some peasant women coming out of the Catholic church discussing aloud—apparently for my benefit—how they would deal with spies. Even if the authorities released the spy, the peasants would put his eyes out, cut off his tongue, etc. It was clear that we could not remain in Poronin after Ilyich was set free. I began packing up, sorting out things that we must take along, and those that we might leave in Poronin. Our household went to pieces. Our servant, whom we had to hire for the summer because of mother's illness, had been telling the neighbours all kinds of fables about us, about our connections with Russia, so I managed to ship her off as fast as I could to Cracow, where she yearned to go, paying her fare and wages in advance. Our neighbour's little girl helped us to tend the stove and buy provisions. My mother—she was already 72 years old—was very ill. She saw that something was wrong but could not understand just what it was. Although I had told her that Vladimir Ilyich was under arrest, at times she would say that he had been drafted for the war. She became agitated every time I left the house, thinking I would disappear in the same way as Vladimir Ilyich. Tichomirnov, who lived with us, kept on smoking pensively and packing books. Once I had to get a certain certificate from the same peasant-witness whom the *gendarme*-officer had made fun of when our house was searched. I went to see him in his house at the end of the village, a typical poor-peasant's house, and we had a long talk about the war, about the people who were fighting in the war, and those who were interested in it. He then saw me home in a friendly manner.

Finally, the pressure exerted by the deputy from Vienna, Victor Adler, and the Lvov deputy Diamond, who both vouched for Vladimir Ilyich, had its effect. On August 19th Vladimir Ilyich was released. I went to Novy Targ in the morning as usual, but this time I was even admitted into the prison to help gather up Ilyich's things. We hired a cart and went to Poronin. There we were forced to stay for another week before we succeeded in getting a permit to move to Cracow. In Cracow we went to the same landlady from whom Kamenev and Inessa had once rented rooms. Half the house had been converted into a military hospital, but she managed to find a nook for us. She had not much time for us, by the way. A battle had been fought recently at Krasnik in which two of her sons had participated, and she had no news from them.

On the next day we witnessed a horrible scene from the window of our room. A train had arrived from Krasnik, bringing dead and wounded soldiers. Relatives of the men who had taken part in the battle ran after the stretcher-bearers and looked into the faces of the dead and dying, afraid to recognise their kin. Those who had been less seriously wounded came slowly from the railway station, with bandaged heads and arms. People who met the train helped them carry their baggage, offered them food and jugs of beer obtained from near-by restaurants. One could not help thinking: "Here it is war!" And this was only the first battle.

In Cracow it did not take us long to obtain permission to go abroad to a neutral country, Switzerland. We had some matters to arrange. Not long before this my mother had become a "capitalist." Her sister, a school teacher, died in Novotcherkask and left her all her property—silver spoons, icons, some dresses and four thousand rubles saved up in the course of thirty years of teaching. The money was deposited in a Cracow bank. To get it from there it was necessary to resort to the services of a banker in Vienna who obtained the money, retaining exactly half of it for his services. During the war we lived mainly on this money, with such economy that when we came back to Russia in 1917 some of it was still left, and this sum, taken from us during a raid in Petersburg in July 1917, was offered as evidence that Vladimir Ilyich had received money from the German government as a reward for espionage.

It took us a whole week to travel from Cracow to

the Swiss frontier. We stopped for long periods at railway stations to let military trains pass. We observed the chauvinist agitation conducted by nuns and other women grouped around them. At the railway stations they distributed small images, prayer books and similar articles among the soldiers. Smartly dressed military men were at all railway stations. The cars were decorated with various slogans as to what to do with the French, the English, the Russians: "jedem Russ ein Schuss!" (a shot for every Russian!). At one of the sidings stood several cars loaded with insect powder; the cars were destined for the front.

In Vienna we stopped for a day to get the necessary papers, to arrange money matters, to telegraph to Switzerland for someone to vouch for us, so that we might enter the country. We were vouched for by Greulich, oldest member of the Swiss Social-Democratic Party. In Vienna, Riazanov took Vladimir Ilyich to see Victor Adler who had helped to secure Ilyich's release. Adler told us of his conversation with the Minister. The latter had asked: "Are you certain that Ulyanov is an enemy of the Tsarist government?"—"Oh, yes," Adler answered, "a more implacable enemy than your Excellency." From Vienna to the Swiss frontier we proceeded quite rapidly.

BERNE (1914-15)

On September 5th we finally entered Switzerland and went to Berne.

We were not yet finally decided where we would live, in Geneva or Berne. Ilyich was drawn to the old hearth, to his accustomed spot in Geneva where it used to be so convenient to work at the "Société de Lecture," which had a good Russian library. But our friends in Berne maintained that Geneva had changed considerably and was crowded with exiles from other cities and from France, and that the usual emigré atmosphere pervaded there. Without deciding the matter definitely, we took a room in Berne for the time being.

Ilyich began corresponding with Geneva to ascertain whether any people were going to Russia—they had to be utilised for establishing contact with Russia; he inquired whether there was still a Russian printing office in Geneva and whether it would be possible to publish Russian leaflets, etc., there.

On the day following our arrival from Galicia a conference was held of all the Bolsheviks present at that time in Berne—Shklovsky, the Safarovs, the Duma-deputy Samoilov, Mokhov and others. At that conference, held in the woods, Ilyich expounded his views on current events. As a result of the conference a resolution was adopted characterising the war as an imperialist predatory war and branding the conduct of the leaders of the Second International who had voted for war credits as treason to the cause of the proletariat.

The resolution stated that "from the standpoint of the working class and the toiling masses of all *Russian* nationalities in Russia the lesser evil would be a defeat of the tsarist monarchy and its armies which oppress Poland, the Ukraine and a number of nationalities in Russia." The resolution launched the slogan of conducting propaganda in all countries for a Socialist revolution, civil war and a determined struggle against chauvinism and patriotism in all countries without exception. At the same time the

resolution outlined a programme of action for Russia:
struggle against the monarchy, propaganda for
revolution, struggle for a republic, for the emancipation of nationalities oppressed by the "Great
Russians," for the confiscation of the estates of the
nobility and for the eight-hour day.

The Berne resolution was in its substance a chal-
lenge to the entire capitalist world. The Berne
resolution was, of course, not written for the purpose
of being pigeon-holed. It was first of all sent to all
Bolshevik sections abroad. Then Samoilov took the
thesis with him for discussion with the Russian part
of the Central Committee and with the Duma fraction. It was not yet certain what position they took.
Connections with Russia were interrupted. Only
later it became known that the Russian part of the
Central Committee and the Bolshevist part of the
Duma fraction struck the right note from the very
outset. For the advanced workers of our country,
for our Party organisation the resolutions of international congresses about war were not merely scraps
of paper, they were guides to action.

During the very first days of the war, when mobilisation was declared, the St. Petersburg Committee
issued a leaflet with the slogan: "Down with War!
War against War!" A number of industrial enterprises in St. Petersburg declared a strike on the day
the reserves were mobilised, and an effort was even
made to hold a demonstration. But the war called
forth such an orgy of mob-patriotism and military
reaction was so greatly strengthened that not much
could be accomplished. Our Duma fraction firmly
held to the line of struggle against war, the line of
continued struggle against the tsarist rule. This
firmness created an impression even upon the Mensheviks, and the Social-Democratic fraction as a

whole adopted a resolution which was read from the Duma tribune. The resolution was couched in cautious terms, much was left unsaid; still, it was a resolution of protest and aroused general indignation among the rest of the members of the Duma. The indignation increased when the Social-Democratic fraction (still as a whole) abstained from voting on war credits and left the Chamber in a body as a demonstration of protest. The Bolshevist organisation quickly went deep underground, began issuing leaflets with instructions on how to utilise the war in the interests of developing and deepening the revolutionary struggle. Anti-war propaganda was started in the provinces. Reports from the localities indicated that the propaganda found support among the revolutionary-minded workers. Of all this we learned abroad much later.

In our groups abroad, which had not experienced the revolutionary upsurge of the preceding months in Russia, and were weary of the emigré atmosphere from which they sought to escape at all costs, there was not the firmness shown by our Duma deputies, and by the Russian Bolshevist organisations.

In Paris our Bolshevist group wavered. Although the majority of the group expressed themselves against the war and against volunteering, some of the comrades—Sapozhkov (Kuznetsov), Kazakov (Britman, Svyagin), Misha Edisherov (Davidov), Moisseyev (Ilya, Zefir) and others joined the French army as volunteers. The Bolshevik, the Menshevik and Socialist-Revolutionary volunteers (about 80 in all) adopted a declaration in the name of the "Russian Republicans," which was published in the French press. Before the volunteers left Paris Plekhanov made a farewell speech in their honour.

The majority of the Paris group condemned

volunteering. But even the other groups were not clear on the question. Vladimir Ilyich realised that at such a serious moment it was particularly important that every Bolshevik should ponder over the significance of the events that were taking place; a comradely interchange of opinion was necessary; it was not expedient to fix every shade of opinion at once, at the very outset. It was necessary to come to a complete understanding. This is why, in answering Karpinsky's letter stating the view-point of the Geneva section, Ilyich wrote: "Would it not be better to make this 'criticism' and my 'anti-criticism' a subject for discussion."

Ilyich knew that in a comradely discussion it would be easier to arrive at an understanding than through correspondence. But of course the times were not such as would permit the matter to be limited to comradely discussions in a narrow circle of Bolsheviks.

Early in October it became known that upon his return from Paris Plekhanov had delivered a lecture in Geneva and was preparing to deliver a lecture at Lausanne.

Plekhanov's position troubled Vladimir Ilyich. He both believed and did not believe that Plekhanov had turned *oboronetz*.* "It is simply impossible to believe," he would say, and add pensively: "it must be the effect of Plekhanov's military past!" When on October 10th a telegram came from Lausanne to the effect that the lecture was scheduled for the next day, the 11th, Ilyich got busy preparing for the lecture, and I tried to free him from other affairs, to arrange with our people as to who would go from Berne, etc. We were quite settled in Berne. At that

* Literally "defensist," i.e. in favour of national defence in the war.—Ed.

time the Zinovievs also lived there, having arrived two weeks after us. Inessa, too, lived in Berne.

I could not go to the lecture, and was told about it in detail later. But having read in the *Notes of the Lenin Institute* F. Ilyin's memoirs about that lecture, and knowing what it meant at that time to Ilyich, I can picture to myself quite vividly what happened. Inessa, too, later related to me what occurred. Our people came to the lecture from all over. From Berne—Zinoviev, Inessa, Shklovsky from Bojio-on-the-Clarant, Krylenko, Bukharin, and, of course, the comrades from Lausanne.

Ilyich feared that he might not be able to get in to hear Plekhanov's lecture, to say all the things he had to say; the Mensheviks might not admit so many Bolsheviks. I could quite understand his not wanting to talk to people about all sorts of inconsequential things at that time and I remember the naïve ruses he resorted to in order to remain alone. I clearly recall how, amidst the bustle of the dinner table at the Movshoviches one day, Ilyich was so absorbed in himself, so agitated, that he could not swallow a bite. One can understand the somewhat forced jest Ilyich expressed to the comrades sitting beside him in the hall, when Plekhanov, in his introductory remarks, said something to the effect that he had not expected to speak before such a large audience. "Zhulyabia" ("bunk"), Ilyich muttered and gave himself up entirely to hearing what Plekhanov had to say. With the first part of the lecture in which Plekhanov attacked the Germans, Ilyich was in agreement and he applauded. In the second part, Plekhanov developed the defence of fatherland point of view. There could no longer be any doubt as to where Plekhanov stood. Ilyich asked for the floor. No one else did. Carrying a glass of beer in his hand he approached the speaker's table. He spoke calmly, and only the pallor of his face betrayed his excitement. In his speech he said in effect that the outbreak of the war was no accident, that the whole nature of the development of bourgeois society had laid the basis for the war. The International Socialist Congresses—at Stuttgart, Copenhagen and Basle had laid down what the attitude of Socialists was to be toward impending war. The Social-Democrats would be fulfilling their duty only when they waged a struggle against the chauvinist intoxication in their own countries. It was necessary to turn the war, which had just begun, into a conflict between the proletariat and the ruling class.

Ilyich had only ten minutes. He expressed only the essentials. Plekhanov, with his usual sharpness of wit, made the rebuttal. The Mensheviks—they were in an overwhelming majority—applauded him violently. The impression was created that Plekhanov was victorious.

On October 14th, three days later, in the same place where Plekhanov had delivered his lecture—in the Maison du Peuple (People's House), Ilyich was scheduled to deliver a lecture. The hall was packed. The lecture was successful, Ilyich was in high, militant spirits. He fully developed his view-point concerning the war as an imperialist war. He pointed out that in Russia a leaflet had already been issued by the Central Committee against the war, that a similar leaflet had been issued by the Caucasian organisation and other groups. The best Socialist paper in Europe at that time, he said, was *Golos* (*The Voice*) to which Martov contributed: "I have often strongly disagreed with Martov," he said. "All the more definitely therefore must I say that this writer at present is doing what a Social-Democrat should do. He criticises his own government, he exposes the bourgeoisie in his own country, he rails against his ministers."

In private conversation Ilyich more than once remarked how good it would be if Martov came over to our side. But he did not believe that Martov would long remain in the position he had taken. He knew how easily Martov fell under other people's influence. "He writes so while he is alone," Ilyich added. Ilyich's lecture was a tremendous success. He repeated this lecture, "The Proletariat and the War," later, at Geneva.

When he returned from his lecture trip Ilyich found a letter from Shlyapnikov informing him from Stockholm of the work in Russia, of Vandervelde's telegram to the Social-Democratic fraction in the Duma and of the replies of the Menshevist and Bolshevist deputies. When war was declared Emile Vandervelde, Belgian delegate on the International Socialist Bureau, accepted a ministerial post in the Belgian government. Not long before the war he had been in Russia and saw the struggle that the workers of Russia waged against the tsarist autocracy, but had not understood its depth. Vandervelde telegraphed to both groups of the Social-Democratic Duma fraction, calling upon the fraction to help the Russian government conduct a determined war against Germany.

The Menshevist deputies who at first refused to vote for war credits wavered considerably when they learned of the position taken by the majority of the Socialist parties, and so their reply to Vandervelde showed a complete change of front. They declared that they would not oppose the war. The Bolshevist fraction sent a reply vigorously rejecting any suggestion of supporting the war and discontinuing the struggle against the tsarist government. Much was left unsaid in the reply, but the basic line was correctly laid down. The importance of maintaining contact with Russia was evident, and Ilyich more strongly than ever insisted that Shlyapnikov remain in Stockholm and strengthen connections with the Duma fraction and the Russians in general. This could best be accomplished through Stockholm.

As soon as Ilyich came to Berne from Cracow he wrote Karpinsky, inquiring whether it would be possible to print a leaflet in Geneva. The theses adopted during the first days after our arrival in Berne were, by a decision taken a month later, to be recast and published in the form of a manifesto. Ilyich renewed the correspondence with Karpinsky about publishing the leaflet, sending letters by trusted messengers as occasion offered and keeping the matter very secret. At that time it was not yet clear what position the Swiss government would take toward anti-militarist propaganda.

On the next day after receiving Shlyapnikov's letter Vladimir Ilyich wrote to Karpinsky:

"Dear K: While I was in Geneva *glad* news came from Russia. The text of the reply of the Russian Social-Democrats to Vandervelde also arrived. We therefore decided instead of a separate manifesto to publish a paper to be called the *Sotsial Demokrat*, Central Organ. . . . By Monday we will send you some slight corrections to the manifesto and a *different* signature (for after communication with Russia we are coming out officially)."

At the end of October Ilyich again went on a lecture tour, first visiting Montreux and then Zurich. At his Zurich lecture Trotsky spoke and was indignant because Ilyich had called Kautsky "traitor." And Ilyich had deliberately put every question in the sharpest manner in order to bring our clearly everyone's position. The struggle with the defensists was in full swing.

This struggle was not merely an internal Party struggle and touched not only Russian matters. It was a struggle of international character.

"The Second International died, vanquished by opportunism," Ilyich maintained. It was necessary to gather forces for the Third International, purged of opportunism.

But what forces could be relied upon?

The only Social-Democratic members of Parliament who refused to vote for war credits besides the Russians were the Serbians. There were only two in the Skupshtshina (Serbian Parliament). In Germany, on the outbreak of the war, all the Social-Democratic members of the Reichstag voted for war credits, but as early as September 10th Karl Liebknecht, F. Mehring, Rosa Luxemburg and Clara Zetkin drew up a declaration of protest against the position taken by the majority of the German Social-Democrats. This declaration they succeeded in publishing in the Swiss newspapers only at the end of October, and in the German press they could not publish it at all. Of the German papers the Bremen *Burgerzeitung* from the very beginning of the war took the furthest position to the left, stating on August 23rd that the "proletarian international" was destroyed. In France the Socialist Party with Guesde and Vaillant at the head slipped into chauvinism. But in the lower ranks of the Party anti-war sentiment was quite widespread. For the Belgian party Vandervelde's conduct was typical. In England the chauvinism of Hyndman and the British Socialist Party was opposed by MacDonald and Keir Hardie of the opportunist Independent Labour Party. In the neutral countries there was anti-war sentiment, but it was mainly of a pacifist nature. The most revolutionary was the Italian Socialist Party with its paper *Avanti* at the head; it combatted chauvinism and exposed the predatory aims that were behind the appeals for war. It was supported by the great majority of the advanced workers. On September 27th an Italo-Swiss Socialist Conference took place at Lugano. Our theses on the war were sent to this conference. The conference characterised the war as an imperialist war and called upon the international proletariat to fight for peace.

In general, the voices against chauvinism, the international voices, still sounded weak, disjointed, uncertain, but Ilyich did not doubt that they would grow stronger and stronger. During the entire autumn he was in high militant spirits.

The memory of that autumn is interwoven in my mind with the autumnal scene of the forest at Berne. The autumn of that year was a glorious one. We lived in Berne on Distelweg, a small, tidy, quiet street adjoining the Berne forest which extended for several kilometres. Across the road lived Inessa, five minutes' walk—the Zinovievs, ten minutes' walk— the Shklovskys. We would wander for hours along the forest roads, bestrewn with fallen yellow leaves. On most occasions the three of us went together on these walks, Vladimir Ilyich, Inessa and myself. Vladimir Ilyich would develop his plans of the international struggle. Inessa took it all very much to heart. In this unfolding struggle she began to take a most direct part, conducting correspondence, translating our documents into French and English, gathering materials, talking with people, etc. Sometimes we would sit for hours on the sunlit-wooded mountain-side while Ilyich jotted down outlines of his speeches and articles and polished his formulations; I studied Italian with the aid of a Toussain text-book, Inessa sewed a skirt and basked with delight in the autumnal sun—she had not yet fully recovered from the effects of her imprisonment. In the evening we would all gather in Gregory's (Zinoviev's) little room (the three of them, Gregory, Lilina and their little boy Styopa lived in one room) and after a little bantering with Styopa before the boy went to sleep, Ilyich would make a series of concrete proposals.

The main points of the line of struggle Ilyich formulated in a condensed, precise manner in his letter to Shlyapnikov of October 17th:

". . . . Kautsky is now *more harmful than all of them*. No words can describe how dangerous and mean are his sophisms which cover up the rascality of the opportunists (in the *Neue Zeit* [*New Era*]) with smooth and slick phrases. The opportunists are an open evil; the German centre with Kautsky at its head a hidden evil embellished for diplomatic purposes and dulling the eyes, the intelligence, and the consciousness of the workers, is more dangerous than anything else. Our task at present is a determined and open struggle against international opportunism and those who shield it (Kautsky). This is what we are going to do in the Central Organ which we shall soon issue (probably two pages). One must exert every effort to uphold the just hatred of the class-conscious workers for the hideous conduct of the Germans; one must draw from this hatred political conclusions against opportunism and against every concession to opportunism. This is an international task. It devolves upon us; there is nobody else. One cannot shirk it. The slogan of 'simply' re-establishing the International is incorrect (because the danger of a spineless conciliatory resolution along the line of Kautsky and Vandervelde is very, very great!). The slogan of 'peace' is incorrect, as the slogan must be: changing the national war into civil war. (This change may take a long time, it may and will demand a number of preliminary conditions, but all the work must be conducted *along the line of such* a change, in this spirit and in this direction.) Not the sabotaging of the war, not undertaking sporadic individual acts in this direction, but conducting mass propaganda (and not only among 'civilians') it is that leads to the transformation of the war into civil war.

"In Russia, chauvinism hides behind phrases about *La Belle France* and unfortunate Belgium (how about the Ukraine and others?), or behind the 'popular' hatred for the Germans (and 'Kaiserism'). It is therefore our absolute duty to struggle against these sophisms. In order that the struggle may proceed along a definite and clear line, one must have a slogan that summarises it. This slogan is: For us *Russians*, from the point of view of the interests of the labouring masses and the working class of *Russia*, there can not be the slightest doubt, absolutely no doubt whatever, that the *lesser* evil would be, here and now, the defeat of tsarism in the present war. For tsarism is a hundred times worse than Kaiserism. We do not sabotage the war, but we struggle against chauvinism, all propaganda and agitation being directed towards international unification (drawing together, expressing solidarity, reaching agreements *selon les circonstances*)* of the proletariat in the interests of civil war. It would also be erroneous both to appeal for *individual* acts of firing at officers, and to

* According to circumstances.—Ed.

allow arguments like the one which says: We do not want to help Kaiserism. The former is a deviation towards anarchism, the latter towards opportunism. As to ourselves, we must prepare a mass (at least a collective) action in the army, not of one nation alone, and conduct *all* the work of propaganda and agitation in this direction. To direct the work (stubborn, systematic work that may require a long time) in the spirit of transforming the national war into civil war—this is the whole issue. The moment for such a transformation is a different question; at present it is not yet clear. We must allow this moment to ripen, we must systematically 'force it to ripen.' . . . The peace slogan is in my judgment incorrect at the present moment. This is a philistine's, a preacher's, slogan. The proletarian slogan must be civil war.

"Objectively, from the fundamental change in the situation of Europe, there follows such a slogan for the epoch of mass war. The same slogan follows from the Basle resolution.

"We can neither 'promise' civil war nor 'decree it,' but it is our duty to work *in this direction,* if need be, for a very long time. You will find details in the article in the Central Organ."*

Two and a half months after the beginning of the war, Ilyich had already hammered out a clear, distinct line of struggle. This line guided all of his subsequent activity. The international range of his activity gave a new tone to his work for Russia, it gave it fresh vigour, new colour. Had it not been for the many years of hard work previously given to building the Party, to organising the working class of Russia, Ilyich would not have been able so quickly and so firmly to take a correct line with respect to the

* *Collected Works*, Vol. XVIII, pp. 73-75.

new problems raised by the imperialist war. Had
he not been in the thick of the international struggle,
he would not have been able so firmly to lead the
Russian proletariat towards the October victory.

Number 33 of the *Sotsial-Demokrat* was published
on November 1st, 1914. At first only 500 copies were
printed, but later it was found necessary to print
another 1,000. On November 14th Ilyich joyfully
informed Karpinsky that the paper had been delivered to one of the points not far from the border
and that soon it would be shipped farther.

With the aid of Naine and Graber a resumé of the
manifesto was published on November 13th in *La
Sentinelle*, a Swiss newspaper, published in French in
the workers' centre of Chaux-de-Fonds. Ilyich was
jubilant. We sent translations of the manifesto to
French, English and German newspapers.

For the purpose of developing propaganda among
the French, Vladimir Ilyich communicated with
Karpinsky about arranging in Geneva a lecture to
be delivered in French by Inessa. He wrote to
Shlyapnikov about addressing the Swedish congress.
Shlyapnikov did address it and very successfully.
Thus little by little the "international action" of the
Bolsheviks was unfolded.

As regards connections with Russia the situation
was not so good. Shlyapnikov sent some interesting
material from St. Petersburg for No. 34 of the paper,
but along with it we had to publish in that issue the
news about the arrest of the five Bolshevik Duma
deputies. The connection with Russia again became
weaker.

While developing a passionate struggle against the
betrayal of the cause of the proletariat by the Second
International, Ilyich at the same time began, immediately upon his arrival in Berne, preparing an

essay on "Karl Marx"* for *Granat's Encyclopedic Dictionary*. In this essay he begins by explaining his exposition of the teachings of Marx with an explanation of his philosophy, dividing it into two parts: "Philosophic Materialism" and "Dialectics," and then, after explaining Marx's economic theories, he shows how Marx approached the question of Socialism and the tactics of the class struggle of the proletariat.

This was not the usual way of presenting Marx's teachings. Before writing the chapters on philosophic materialism and dialectics Ilyich again diligently reread Hegel and other philosophers and continued these studies even after he had finished the essay. The aim of his work in the realm of philosophy was to master the method of transforming philosophy into a concrete guide to action. His brief remarks about the dialectical approach toward all phenomena, made in 1921 in the course of the controversies with Trotsky and Bukharin concerning the trade unions, are the best evidence of how much Ilyich had gained in this respect from his studies in philosophy begun upon his arrival in Berne and constituting a continuation of what he had accomplished in the matter of philosophic studies in 1908-09, when he fought with the *Machists*.

Struggle and study, study and scientific work were always for Ilyich strongly bound together. Although at first sight they may have appeared to be only parallel work, there was always the closest and most profound connection between them.

In the beginning of 1915 the strenuous work of consolidating the Bolshevist groups abroad was continued. Although a definite understanding had already been reached among them the times were

* Published separately in the Little Lenin Library.—Ed.

such that a cemented whole was needed more than ever. Before the war the centre of the Bolshevist groups, the so-called Committee of Organisations Abroad, had had its headquarters in Paris. Now the centre had to be moved to Switzerland, a neutral country, to Berne, where the editorial board of the Central Organ was located. Agreement had to be reached on all points—the appraisal of the war, the new tasks confronting the Party, the ways of meeting them; the work of the groups had to be made more exact. The Bojio group, for instance (Krylenko, Bukharin, Rozmirovich) decided to publish their own organ abroad, the *Zvezda* (*Star*), and they went about it in such a hurried fashion that they did not even arrange the matter with the Central Organ. We learned about this plan from Inessa. Such a publication was to little purpose. There was no money even to publish the Central Organ, and although there were no differences of opinion so far, such might easily arise. Any incautious phrase might be caught up by opponents and exaggerated in every way. It was necessary to keep in step. Such were the times.

At the end of February a conference of all groups abroad was called in Berne. Besides the Swiss groups there was the group from Paris. The Parisians sent Grisha Belenky, who reported in detail about the defensist sentiments which prevailed in the Paris group in the beginning of the war. The Londoners could not come and assigned their mandate to a proxy. The Bojio group were hesitant about attending, and came only toward the end. Together with them came the "Japanese," our nickname for the Kievites, Comrades Piatakov and Bosche (sister of E. F. Rozmirovich) who had escaped from Siberia by way of Japan and America. That was the time when we clutched convulsively at every new person who was at one with our idea. The "Japanese" made a good impression on us. Their arrival undoubtedly strengthened our forces abroad.

The conference adopted a clear-cut resolution on the war; there was a debate on the slogan of a United States of Europe (opposed with particular heat by Inessa); the character of the work of the groups abroad was mapped out; it was decided not to publish the paper at Bojio. A new Committee of Organisations Abroad was elected, consisting of the Berne comrades Shklovsky, Kaparov, Inessa, Lilina and Krupskaya.

The task of the day was to rally our forces on an international scale. The difficulty of this task was made apparent by the Inter-Allied Socialist Conference, consisting of representatives of the Socialist Parties in England, Belgium, France, and Russia which took place in London on February 14th, 1914. The conference was summoned by Vandervelde, but it was organised by the English Independent Labour Party headed by Keir Hardie and MacDonald. Before the conference they had been opposed to the war, and for international unity. At first the Independent Labour Party considered inviting delegates from Germany and Austria, but the French declared that they would not participate in the conference under such circumstances. There were 11 delegates from England, 16 from France, 3 from Belgium. Three Socialist-Revolutionaries came from Russia, and there was one delegate from the Menshevist Organisation Committee. We were to be represented there by Litvinov. One could foresee what kind of conference it would be, what results it would bring, and it was therefore agreed that Litvinov should merely read the declaration of our Central Committee. Ilyich drew up an outline of this declaration

for Litvinov. It contained the demand that Vandervelde, Guesde and Sembat resign at once from the
bourgeois cabinets of Belgium and France and that
all the Socialist parties support the Russian workers
in their struggle against tsarism. The declaration
stated that the Social-Democrats of Germany and
Austria had committed a monstrous crime against
Socialism and the International by voting war
credits and concluding "civil peace" with the
Junkers, priests and bourgeoisie, but that the
Belgian and the French Socialists had acted no
better. The declaration continued: "The workers
of Russia extend their comradely hand to the Socialist
who acts like Karl Liebknecht, like the Socialists of
Serbia and Italy, like the British comrades in the
Independent Labour Party and certain members of
the British Socialist Party, like our arrested comrades
of the Russian Social-Democratic Labour Party.

"We call upon you to take this road, the road of
Socialism. Down with chauvinism that ruins the
proletarian cause! Long live international Socialism!"

These were the concluding words of the declaration. It was signed by the Central Committee and
also by Berzin, representing the Lettish Social-
Democrats. The chairman did not allow Litvinov
to read the declaration to the end, and so he handed
it to the chairman and left the conference declaring
that the Russian Social-Democratic Labour Party
would not participate in it. After Litvinov's departure the conference adopted a resolution which
declared support for the "war of liberation" until
victory over Germany was achieved. Keir Hardie
and MacDonald also voted for this resolution.

At the same time preparations were going on for
an international women's conference. It was, of

course, important not only that such a conference should take place, but also that it should not be of a pacifist character, and that it should take a definitely revolutionary position. This necessitated much preliminary work, most of which fell to Inessa. As she usually assisted the editors of the Central Organ in translating various documents and had been a participant in the struggle developing against "defensism" from the very beginning, Inessa was very well fitted for this work. Besides, she knew languages. She corresponded with Clara Zetkin, Balabanova, Kollontai, with English women, thus strengthening the threads of the international ties. These threads were very feeble, were constantly breaking, but Inessa kept sturdily at her task. Through Stahl, who lived in Paris, she conducted correspondence with the French comrades. It was easiest of all to communicate with Balabanova. She worked in Italy, and helped to publish the *Avanti*. This was the period when the revolutionary spirit of the Italian Socialist Party was at its height. In Germany anti-defensist sentiments were spreading. On December 2nd Karl Liebknecht voted against war credits. The International Women's Conference was summoned by Clara Zetkin. She was the secretary of the International Bureau of Socialist Women. Together with Karl Liebknecht, Rosa Luxemburg and F. Mehring she fought against the chauvinist majority in the German Social-Democratic Party. It was with her that Inessa communicated. Kollontai had left the Mensheviks about that time. In January she wrote to Vladimir Ilyich and myself, enclosing a leaflet. "My esteemed and dear comrade," Vladimir Ilyich wrote her in return, "I am very grateful to you for sending the leaflet; at present I can only hand it over to the local members of the editorial body of *Rabotnitsa* (*The Working Woman*). They have already sent a letter to Zetkin, apparently of the same content as yours." And then Vladimir Ilyich proceeded to explain the position of the Bolsheviks. "Apparently you do not entirely agree with the slogan of civil war and assign it, so to speak, a subordinate (and perhaps even a conditional) place to the slogan of peace. And you emphasise that 'we must put forward a *slogan that would unite all*.' I will tell you frankly that the thing I fear most at the present time is indiscriminate unity, which, I am convinced, is most dangerous and harmful to the proletariat." It was against the background of Ilyich's position that Inessa conducted her correspondence with Kollontai concerning the conference. Kollontai did not succeed in getting to the conference.

The international conference at Berne took place March 26th-28th. The largest and most organised delegation was the German, headed by Clara Zetkin. The delegates of the Russian Central Committee were Armand, Lilina, Ravich, Krupskaya, Rozmirovich. The Polish "Rozlamovists" were represented by Kamenskaya (Domskaya), who supported the delegation of the Central Committee. The Russians had two more delegates representing the Organisation Committee. Balabanova came from Italy. Louise Simanot, a French woman, was very much under the influence of Balabanova. The Dutch were in a purely pacifist mood. Rolland-Holst, who then belonged to the left wing, could not come; a delegate came from the Troelstra* Party which was thoroughly chauvinist. The English delegates belonged to the opportunist Independent Labour Party, the Swiss delegates were also pacifistically inclined. In fact, pacifism was the pre-

---

* Troelstra was then leader of the Socialist Party of Holland.—Ed.

dominant mood. Of course, if we bear in mind the London Conference a month and a half earlier, this one marked a considerable step forward. The very fact that the conference consisted of delegates from countries at war with one another was significant.

The majority of the German women belonged to the Karl Liebknecht-Rosa Luxemburg group. This group had begun to dissociate itself from the chauvinists and to fight its government. Rosa Luxemburg had already been arrested. But this was at home. At the international conference they thought they had to be as conciliatory as possible because they were the delegation from a country which at the moment was winning victories on the battle-front. If the conference, assembled after so much effort, went to pieces, they thought, all the blame would be placed on them; the chauvinists of all countries, and the German social-patriots above all, would rejoice at the collapse of the conference. Therefore Clara Zetkin was ready to make concessions to the pacifists, which meant watering down the revolutionary content of the resolutions. Our delegation—the delegation of the Central Committee of the Russian Social-Democratic Labour Party, assumed the standpoint of Ilyich, as expressed in the letter to Kollontai. The aim was not to achieve indiscriminate unity, but unity for the revolutionary struggle against chauvinism, for the merciless revolutionary struggle of the proletariat against the ruling class. There was no condemnation of chauvinism in the resolution drawn up by the commission consisting of the Germans, English and Dutch. We brought forward our own declaration. It was defended by Inessa. The Polish representative Kamenskaya also spoke in support of it. We remained alone. On all sides our "splitting" policy was denounced. But events soon proved the correctness of our position. The goody-goody pacifism of the English and the Dutch did not advance international action a single step. The important rôle in hastening the end of the war was played by the revolutionary struggle and rupture with the chauvinists.

Ilyich ardently devoted himself to the mobilisation of the forces for the struggle on the international front. "It does not matter that we now number only a few individuals," he once remarked, "millions will be with us." He drew up our resolution for the Berne Women's Conference and followed all its work. But one felt how difficult it was for him to remain in the rôle of a leader behind the scenes in a matter of such great importance that was taking place right in the vicinity and in which he so ardently longed to take a direct part.

I remember one incident: Inessa and I were sitting in the hospital at the bedside of Abram Skovno, who had undergone an operation. Ilyich came in and immediately began to urge Inessa to go at once to Zetkin and persuade her of the correctness of our position; she ought to understand, he said, she could not fail to understand that at a time like this we must not slip into pacifism; all questions must be presented in the sharpest manner. And he continued to pile argument on argument that Inessa was to use to convince Zetkin. Inessa did not want to go, she thought that nothing would come of it. Ilyich insisted, and warmly pleaded with her to go. The conversation between Zetkin and Inessa did not take place, however.

On April 17th there was another international conference at Berne—a conference of Socialist youth. In Switzerland at that time there were considerable numbers of young men from various belligerent countries, who did not want to go to the front and take part in the imperialist war; they had emigrated to a neutral country, Switzerland. Naturally, these young men were permeated with revolutionary sentiment. It is not an accident that the International Women's Conference was followed by the Conference of Socialist Youth.

In the name of the Central Committee of our Party Inessa and Safarov participated in that conference.

In March my mother died. She had been a close comrade, helping in all our work. In Russia, during raids, she would hide illegal materials; she would visit comrades in prison and deliver messages; she had lived with us in Siberia and abroad, managing the household, taking care of arriving or departing comrades, sewing "armour" on special skirts and waistcoats in which illegal literature was concealed, writing "skeletons" of letters between the lines of which our messages were written with invisible ink, etc. The comrades loved her. The last winter was a very trying one for her. All her strength gave out. She was yearning to go to Russia, but we had no one there to care for her. She often argued with Vladimir Ilyich, but she was always solicitous about him, and Vladimir, too, was attentive to her. Once mother was in low spirits. She was an inveterate smoker and had forgotten to buy cigarettes; it was a holiday and tobacco could not be obtained anywhere. When Ilyich saw that, he said: "Don't worry, I'll get some at once." He went searching in the cafés, found cigarettes and brought them to mother. Not long before her death mother once said to me: "No, I won't go alone to Russia, I'll wait until I go with you two." At another time she began speaking about religion. She considered herself religious, but had not been to church for years, never observed religious fasts, never prayed, and in general religion did not play any part whatever in her life, but she never liked to discuss the subject, and now she suddenly said: "I was religious in my youth, but as I lived on and learned life I saw it was all nonsense." More than once she had expressed the desire to be cremated when she died. The little house where we lived was situated quite close to the Berne forest. When the warm spring sun began to shine, mother was drawn to the woods. I went with her, we sat on a bench for a half hour, and then she could hardly get back home. Next day she was already in her death agony. We did as she had requested—cremated her at the Berne Crematorium.

Vladimir Ilyich and I waited at the crematory. In about two hours an attendant brought us a tin can with the ashes still warm and showed us where they were to be buried.

Our family life became still more student-like. Our landlady, a pious old laundress, asked us to look for another room, explaining that she wanted to rent her room to believers. We moved to another room.

On February 10th the trial of the five Duma deputies took place. All the Bolshevik deputies—Petrovsky, Muranov, Badayev, Samoilov, Shagov and also L. B. Kamenev were sentenced to exile.

In the article, "What has the Trial of the Russian Social-Democratic Labour Fraction Proved," March 24th, 1915, Ilyich wrote: "The facts tell us that in the very first months after the beginning of the war, the class-conscious vanguard of the workers of Russia rallied, *in practice*, around the Central Committee and the Central Organ. This fact may be unpleasant to certain 'fractions,' still it cannot be denied. The words quoted in the indictment: 'It is necessary to turn the guns not against our brothers, the wage slaves of other countries, but against the reaction of the bourgeoisie governments and parties of all countries'—these words will spread, thanks to the trial, and they have already spread over Russia as an appeal to proletarian internationalism, to proletarian revolution. The class slogan of the vanguard of the workers of Russia has reached, thanks to the trial, the widest masses of the workers.

"An epidemic of chauvinism among the bourgeoisie and one section of the petty bourgeoisie, vacillations in another section, and a working-class appeal of this nature—this is the actual objective picture of our political divisions. It is to this actual picture, and not to the benevolent wishes of the intelligentsia and founders of little groups, that one has to adapt one's 'prospects,' hopes and slogans.

"The 'Pravdist' papers and the 'Muranov' type* of work have brought about the unity of four-fifths of the class-conscious workers of Russia. About forty thousand workers bought *Pravda*; many more read it. Let war, prison, Siberia, and hard labour break five times more or ten times more—this section of the workers *cannot* be destroyed. It is alive. It is permeated with revolutionary spirit, it is anti-chauvinist. It *alone* stands among the masses of the people, and deeply rooted in their midst, as a protagonist of the internationalism of the toiling, the exploited, the oppressed. It *alone* has kept its ground in the general debacle. It *alone* leads semi-proletarian elements *away from* the social chauvinism of the Cadets, Trudoviks, Plekhanov, *Nasha Zarya*, and on to Socialism. Its existence, its ideas, its work, its appeal to the 'brotherhood of wage slaves of other countries' have been revealed to the whole of

---

* Muranov spoke at the trial on the illegal work of the fraction and the use of parliamentary methods for revolutionary purposes.

Russia by the trial of the Russian Social-Democratic Labour Fraction.

"It is with this section that we must work. It is its unity that must be defended against social chauvinism. It is only along this road that the labour movement of Russia can develop towards social revolution and not towards national liberalism of the 'European' type."*

Events soon proved how completely correct Lenin was. Ilyich worked without interruption for the propaganda of the ideas of internationalism and the exposure of social-chauvinism in all its varied forms.

After mother's death I had a relapse of my ailment, and was ordered by the doctors to the mountains. Ilyich scanned the advertisements for a cheap boarding-house in a non-fashionable locality at the foot of the Rothorn in Soerenberg. We decided on the Marienthal Hotel, and lived there the entire summer.

Shortly before our departure the "Japanese" (Bosche and Piatakov) came to Berne with a plan to publish an illegal magazine abroad, in which it would be possible to discuss thoroughly all the important problems. The *Communist* was to be published under the editorship of the Central Organ, augmented by P. and N. Kievsky (Bosche and Piatakov). This was agreed upon. In the course of the summer Ilyich wrote a long article for the *Communist*, entitled "The Collapse of the Second International." During the same summer Ilyich, together with Zinoviev, prepared, in preparation for the conference of internationalists, a pamphlet entitled *Socialism and War*.

We were quite comfortable at Soerenberg; all

---

* Lenin. *Collected Works*, Vol. XVIII, pp. 155-156. See also Badayev, *The Bolsheviks in the Tsarist Duma.*—Ed.

around there were woods, high mountains, and there was even snow on the peak of the Rothorn. Mail arrived with Swiss punctuality. We discovered that in such an out-of-the-way village as Soerenberg it was possible to obtain free of charge any book from the Berne or Zurich libraries. One sent a post card to the library with one's address and a request to send the book required. No questions asked, no certificates, no guarantees that one would not cheat the library out of the book—a complete contrast to bureaucratic France. Two days later the book arrives, wrapped in cardboard; a ticket is tied to the package, giving on one side the address of the person who requested the book and on the other side—the address of the library that sent the book. This arrangement enabled Ilyich to work in this out-of-the-way place. Ilyich had nothing but praise for Swiss culture. It was very comfortable to work at Soerenberg. Some time later Inessa came to stay with us. We would rise early, and before dinner, which was served at 12 o'clock everywhere in Switzerland, each of us would work in different nooks of the garden. During those hours Inessa often played the piano, and it was particularly good to work to the sounds of the music that reached us. After dinner we sometimes went to the mountains for the rest of the day. Ilyich loved the mountains—he liked to get to the crags of the Rothorn toward evening, when the view above was marvellous and below the fog was turning rosy; or to roam over the Schrattenfluh—there was such a mountain about two kilometres from us—we translated its name "cursed steps." It was impossible to climb to the broad flat summit. The mountain was all covered with some kind of rock corroded by spring streams. We seldom climbed the Rothorn,

M

although from there the view of the Alps was marvellous. We went to bed with the roosters, gathered alpine roses, berries; all of us were ardent mushroom-pickers, there was an abundance of white mushrooms, but there were also many other mushroom varieties, and we argued with so much heat about their classification that one might have thought it was a question of a resolution involving important principles.

In Germany the struggle began to flare up. In April the *International*, a magazine founded by Rosa Luxemburg and Franz Mehring, was published and immediately suppressed. The pamphlet by Junius (Rosa Luxemburg) was published under the title *The Crisis of German Social-Democracy*. An appeal of the German Left Social-Democrats written by Karl Liebknecht, entitled *The Principal Enemy Is In Your Own Country*, was issued, and early in June, K. Liebknecht and Dunker drew up *An Open Letter to the Central Committee of the Social-Democratic Party and the Reichstag Fraction*, protesting against the attitude of the Social-Democratic majority toward the war. This *Open Letter* was signed by a thousand functionaries of the Party.

Noticing the growing influence of the left Social-Democrats, the Central Committee of the German Social-Democratic Party decided to cut across this influence, and issued a manifesto signed by Kautsky, Haase and Bernstein against annexations, and calling for party unity. At the same time it issued another statement in its own name and in the name of the Reichstag fraction against the left opposition.

In Switzerland Robert Grimm called a preliminary conference for June 11th at Berne to discuss the preparations for the international conference of the left-wingers. There were seven persons present at that conference (Grimm, Zinoviev, P. B. Axelrod, Varsky, Valetsky, Balabanova, Morgari). Really, apart from Zinoviev, there were no real left-wingers at that preliminary conference, and the impression one obtained from all the talk was that no one of the participants really wanted to call the conference.

Vladimir Ilyich was very excited and sedulously wrote letters in every direction—to Zinoviev, Radek, Berzin, Kollontai, the comrades at Lausanne, anxious that at the forthcoming conference places should be secured for real left-wingers and that there should be as much solid unity among the lefts as possible. Toward the middle of August the Bolsheviks already had drawn up: 1, a manifesto; 2, resolutions; 3, a draft of a declaration, which were sent to the most pronounced left comrades for consideration and discussion. By October the pamphlet *Socialism and War*, by Lenin and Zinoviev, was already translated into German.

The conference took place September 5th-8th at Zimmerwald. Delegates from eleven countries were present (38 delegates in all). The so-called Zimmerwald Left consisted of only nine (Lenin, Zinoviev, Berzin, Hoeglund, Nerman, Radek, Borchardt, Platten; after the conference Rolland-Holst joined). Of the Russians there were also present at the conference, Trotsky, Axelrod, Martov, Natanson, Chernov, and one Bundist. Trotsky did not join the left Zimmerwaldists.

Vladimir Ilyich went to the conference before it was due to open, and on September 4th, at a private conference, delivered a report concerning the nature of the war, and the tactics to be adopted by the international conference. Debates centred around the question of a manifesto. The Lefts proposed their draft of a manifesto and resolution about the war and the tasks of the Social-Democrats. The majority rejected the draft of the Lefts and adopted a considerably more vague and less militant manifesto. Vladimir Ilyich gives an estimation of the Zimmerwald Conference in his article: "The First Step." The Lefts had signed the general manifesto that was adopted at the Conference, and in this article Ilyich asks: "Was our Central Committee right in signing this manifesto, suffering as it does from lack of consistency, and from timidity?" And he answers: "We think so. That we disagree, that not only our Central Committee but that the whole international Left Wing section of the Conference adhering to the principles of revolutionary Marxism disagrees, is only expressed in a special resolution, in a separate draft manifesto and in a separate declaration on the motives of voting for a compromise manifesto. We did not hide one iota of our views, slogans, tactics. The German edition of our pamphlet, *Socialism and War*, was distributed at the Conference. We have broadcasted, are broadcasting, and shall broadcast our views with no less energy than the manifesto. That this manifesto is taking a *step forward* towards a real struggle against opportunism, towards breaking and splitting with it, is a fact. It would be sectarianism to refuse to take this step *together* with the minority of the German, French, Swedish, Norwegian and Swiss Socialists when we retain full freedom and a full possibility to criticise inconsistency and to struggle for more."*

At the Zimmerwald Conference the Lefts organised their own Bureau and in general formed a distinct group.

Although before the Zimmerwald Conference Ilyich had written that our draft resolution ought to

* See article, "The First Step," *Collected Works*, Vol. XVIII, p. 343.

be presented to the Kautskyites: "The Dutch plus ourselves, plus the Left Germans, plus nought—that does not matter; later it will be not nought but all," he wrote, nevertheless progress was very slow indeed, and Ilyich could not reconcile himself to this. The article, "The First Step," begins precisely with the emphasis on the slow development of the revolutionary movement. "The development of the international Socialist movement proceeds slowly in the epoch of the immense crisis created by the war." Ilyich, therefore, came back from the Zimmerwald Conference in a state of irritation.

The day after Ilyich's arrival from Zimmerwald we climbed the Rothorn. We climbed with a "glorious appetite," but when we reached the summit, Ilyich suddenly lay down on the ground, in an uncomfortable position almost on the snow, and fell asleep. Clouds gathered, then broke; the view of the Alps from the Rothorn was splendid, and Ilyich slept like the dead. He never stirred and slept over an hour. Apparently Zimmerwald had frayed his nerves a good deal and had taken much strength out of him.

It required several days of roaming over the mountains and the atmosphere of Soerenberg before Ilyich was himself again. Kollontai was going to America, and Ilyich wrote urging her to do everything possible to consolidate the American left wing international elements. Early in October we returned to Berne. Ilyich went to Geneva to deliver a lecture on the Zimmerwald Conference, continued to correspond with Kollontai about the Americans, etc.

The autumn was rather sultry. Berne is mainly an administrative and academic town. It has many good libraries, much learning, but life there is

permeated with a kind of petty-bourgeois spirit.
Berne is very "democratic,"—the wife of the highest
official of the Republic shakes her carpets from the
balcony every day, but these carpets, the comforts
of the home, absorb the Berne woman to the utmost.
In the autumn we rented a room fitted with electric
light, moved our valise and our books, and when on
the day we moved the Shklovskys came, I began
showing them how wonderfully the electricity was
burning; but when the Shklovskys left the landlady
burst in and demanded that we move on the very
next day, for she would not tolerate the electricity
being turned on in her house during the day. We
decided that she did not own all the houses, so we
rented another room, more modest, without electricity, and we moved there on the next day. The
petty-bourgeois spirit was dominant and pronounced
throughout Switzerland. A Russian theatrical troupe
playing in German visited Berne; they played L.
Tolstoy's *The Living Corpse*. We went to see the play.
The acting was very good. Ilyich, who hated deeply
every kind of philistinism and conventionality, was
very much moved by that play. The Swiss also liked
the play. But why did the Bernese like it? They
were very sorry for Protasov's wife, they took her
troubles to heart. "She had to marry such a way-
ward husband, they were rich people with a position in society, they could have lived so happily,
poor Lisa!"

In the autumn of 1915 we sat in the libraries more
diligently than ever, we took walks as usual, but all
this could not remove the feeling of being cooped
up in this democratic cage. Somewhere beyond, a
revolutionary struggle was mounting, life was astir,
but it was all so far away.

At Berne little could be accomplished in the matter

of establishing direct connections with the Lefts. I remember Inessa went to French Switzerland to establish contacts with the Swiss Lefts, Naine and Graber, but she could not manage to make an appointment with them. Either Naine was away fishing, or Graber was busy about the house. "Father is busy to-day, it is our washing day, and he is hanging out the washing," Graber's little girl informed Inessa respectfully. Fishing and hanging out washing are not bad occupations; Ilyich more than once stood guard over a pot of milk to keep it from boiling over, but when laundry and the fishing line interfered with talking over important matters about organising the Lefts, it was not so good. Inessa obtained someone else's passport and went to Paris. Upon returning from Zimmerwald, Merrheim and Bourderon had founded a Committee in Paris for the re-establishment of international connections. Inessa went there to represent the Bolsheviks on the Committee. There she had to fight hard for the left line which finally prevailed. She wrote to Vladimir Ilyich in detail about her work. She also did a great deal of work in our Paris group, met a member of the group, Sapozhkov, who had volunteered for the navy but now shared the views of the Bolsheviks and was beginning to conduct propaganda among the French soldiers.

Comrade Shklovsky organised a small chemical laboratory, and our people, Kasparov and Zinoviev, worked there to earn some money. Zinoviev gazed pensively at the tubes and bulbs that now appeared in everyone's room.

At Berne it was possible to do mainly theoretical work. During the year of war many things became clearer. In this connection the question of a United States of Europe is characteristic. In the declaration published by the Central Committee in the Central Organ on November 1st, 1914, we read: "The immediate political slogan of the Social-Democrats of Europe must be the creation of a republican United States of Europe. In contrast to the bourgeoisie which is ready to 'promise' anything in order to draw the proletariat into the general stream of chauvinism, the Social-Democrats will explain that this slogan is false and senseless without the revolutionary overthrow of the German, Austrian and Russian monarchies."*

In March, during the conference of the sections abroad this slogan already gave rise to considerable controversy. In the report of the conference it is stated: ". . . in the question of the slogan, 'United States of Europe,' the discussion took a one-sided political character, and it was decided to postpone the question pending an analysis of the *economic* side of it in the press."†

The question of imperialism, its economic essence, the exploitation of the weaker states by the powerful imperialist states, the exploitation of the colonies, arose in all their magnitude. For this reason the Central Organ came to the conclusion that: "From the point of view of the economic conditions of imperialism, i.e. the export of capital and the division of the world between the 'progressive' and 'civilised' colonial powers, the United States of Europe is under capitalism either impossible or reactionary. . . . A United States of Europe under capitalism amounts to an agreement as to the division of colonies."‡

But perhaps it was possible to advance another

---

* Lenin, *Collected Works*, Vol. XVIII, p. 81.
† *Ibid.*, p. 145.
‡ *Ibid.*, p. 270.

slogan, the slogan of a United States of the World? This is what Ilyich wrote in this connection: "The United States of the World (not of Europe alone) is a state form of national unification and freedom which we connect with Socialism; we think of it as becoming a reality only when the full victory of Communism will have brought about the total disappearance of the state, including its democratic form. As a separate slogan, however, the United States of the World would hardly be a correct one, first, because it coincides with Socialism, second, because it could be erroneously interpreted to mean that the victory of Socialism in one country is impossible; it could also create misconceptions as to the relations of such a country to others."* This article very well reveals the lines along which Ilyich was thinking in 1915. It is clear that he was considering a more profound study of the economic roots of the world war, i.e. of imperialism, on the one hand, and determining the roads which the world struggle for Socialism would take on the other.

It is on these questions that Ilyich worked at the end of 1915 and in 1916, gathering materials for his pamphlet *Imperialism, the Highest Stage of Capitalism*, and re-reading Marx and Engels again and again in order to get a clearer picture of the epoch of the Socialist revolution, its paths and its development.

Zurich (1916)

In January 1916 Vladimir Ilyich began writing his pamphlet on imperialism for the "Parus" publishing

* Lenin, *Collected Works*, Vol. XVIII, pp. 271-72.

house. Ilyich attached tremendous importance to this question, and was of the opinion that it was impossible to give a real, profound appraisal of the war without making completely clear the essence of imperialism, both on its economic and political sides. He therefore willingly undertook this work. In the middle of February, Ilyich found some work to do in the libraries of Zurich, and we went there for a couple of weeks, and then we kept postponing our return until we finally remained in Zurich, which was livelier than Berne. In Zurich there was a considerable number of young foreigners imbued with revolutionary sentiments, there were a lot of workers there, the Social-Democratic Party there was inclined more to the left and there seemed to be less of the petty-bourgeois spirit about the place.

We went to rent a room. We came to a certain Frau Prelog, who looked more Viennese than Swiss, which was to be explained by the fact that she had worked for a long time as a cook in a hotel in Vienna. We settled in her house, but on the next day it appeared that her former tenant was coming back. Someone had cracked his head and he had been in the hospital, and now he was well again. Frau Prelog asked us to find another room, but offered to provide meals for us at very reasonable rates. We ate there for about two months. She served us simple but ample food. Ilyich liked the simplicity of the service, the fact that coffee was served in a cup with a broken handle, that we ate in the kitchen, that the conversation was simple—not about the food, not about the quantity of potatoes to be used for a certain kind of soup, but about matters that were of interest to the boarders. There were not many of them, it is true, and they kept changing. We very soon realised that we had hit upon a peculiar environment, the very "lower depths" of Zurich. For some time a prostitute used to dine at this place, who spoke quite openly about her profession, but what concerned her most was not her profession, but the health of her mother and the kind of work her sister might find. For several days a night-nurse boarded there, then other boarders began to appear. Frau Prelog had a lodger who did not talk much, but from the casual phrases he uttered it was clear that he was of an almost criminal type. No one was embarrassed by our company, and it must be said that in the conversations of those people there was more of the "human," the living element than that heard in the prim dining-rooms of a respectable hotel patronised by well-to-do guests.

I urged Ilyich to change to private board because I feared that with this crowd we might get mixed up in some unpleasant affair. Yet, some of the traits of Zurich's "lower depths" were not without interest.

Later, I read John Reed's *Daughter of the Revolution*, and what I liked particularly was the fact that Reed pictured the prostitutes, not from the standpoint of their profession or of love, but from the standpoint of their other interests. Usually, when the "underworld" is portrayed, little attention is paid to social conditions.

When we were already in Russia Ilyich and I went to see Gorky's *Lower Depths* at the Art Theatre—Ilyich wanted very much to see the play—but he greatly disliked the "theatricality" of the production, the absence of those details of social life which, as the saying goes, "make the music," portray the environment in all its concreteness.

Afterward, every time Ilyich met Frau Prelog in the street he always greeted her in a friendly manner. And we were always meeting her, for we moved to a place near-by, in a narrow alley, staying with the family of a shoemaker named Kammerer. Our room did not quite suit our purpose. The house was an old and sombre one, of construction dating back almost to the sixteenth century, the court was smelly. For the same rent we could have found a better room, but we greatly valued our hosts. It was a worker's family, their outlook was a revolutionary one and they condemned the imperialist war. The place was truly an "international" one: two rooms were occupied by the "landlord," one—by the wife of a German soldier-baker and her children, another by an Italian, a third—by Austrian actors who had a wonderful brown cat, and the fourth—by us Russians. There was no chauvinism in the air, and once when a whole women's international gathered around the gas-stove Frau Kammerer exclaimed indignantly: "The soldiers ought to turn their weapons against their governments!" After that Ilyich would not listen to any suggestions about changing quarters.

From Frau Kammerer I learned a good deal: how to cook satisfying dinners and suppers with the least expenditure of time and money. I also learned something else. Once it was announced in the papers that Switzerland was experiencing difficulties in importing meat and that the government therefore appealed to the citizens to abstain from meat twice a week. The butcher-shops continued selling meat on "meatless" days. I bought meat for dinner as usual, and as I stood by the gas-stove I asked Frau Kammerer what check-up there was to see if the citizens complied with the appeal not to use meat. Were there inspectors going the rounds of the houses?

"But why a check-up?" Frau Kammerer wondered—"once it was published in the papers that there are difficulties, what working man will eat meat on meatless days? Only a bourgeois would do that!" And noticing my embarrassment she added gently: "This does not apply to foreigners." Ilyich was quite captivated by this intelligent proletarian approach.

In looking over my letters to Shlyapnikov for that period I found one dated April 8th, 1915. It characterises the mood of that time. "Dear Friend," I wrote, "I received your letter of April 3rd, and it brought some relief, for it was hard to read your ill-humoured letters in which you promise to leave for America and are ready to make all kinds of accusations. Correspondence is a hideous thing, misunderstandings keep mounting one upon the other. . . . . In the letter that was lost I wrote in detail why it was impossible to drag Gregory either to Russia or to your parts. He took your reproach at not having moved to Stockholm very much to heart. It won't do to ruin the editorial staff of the Central Organ and the foreign base in general. Particularly now the C.O. has with its very teeth gained more than one position during the war. Its editorial staff has played no small part in the International. This must be said point blank, thrusting aside all superfluous modesty. Nor could *The Communist* have appeared without the editorial staff of the Central Organ. It cost no little discussion, care and worry. This applies even more to *Vorbote* (organ of the Zimmerwald Left Group). If the editorial staff is ruined there will be no one to do the work. To get together a new editorial staff is not so easy. Here, every effort was made to get Nikolai Ivanovich, there was talk of his moving to Cracow, then to Berne. Nothing could be done. Even two persons are not enough, and you want to take one away. If you ruin the foreign base, there

will be nothing to send across. At times Gregory gets
devilishly sick of living abroad and he begins to fret.
And you with your reproaches add fuel to the fire.
If we look at the matter from the standpoint of use-
fulness for the work as a whole, then Gregory must
not be touched. The question was raised about
moving the entire editorial department, but this
brought up the question of money, of international
influence, of police considerations. On the question
of money the 'Japanese' stated plainly that they
had none. It is much more expensive to live in
Stockholm, and here Gregory works in a laboratory,
has libraries at his disposal and hence—a chance to
earn at least something by writing. Even here the
question of earnings will become acute for all of us
in the near future.

"As to Ilyich's enthusiasm for emigré affairs, the
reproach is unfounded. He does not at all occupy
himself with these affairs. International matters
take up more time and attention than before, but
this is unavoidable. He is now absorbed, it is true,
with the question of 'self-determination of nations.'
And in my opinion, the best way of 'utilising' him
now is to insist that he write a popular pamphlet
on the subject. The question is least of all academic
at the present time. There is much confusion in the
ranks of the International Social-Democracy on this
question, but this is no reason for putting it off.
During this winter we had discussions on this subject with Radek. I personally got a lot from these
discussions."

In Zurich we lived "quietly," as Ilyich put it in
one of his letters, somewhat removed from the local
colony; we worked regularly and a good deal in the
libraries. After dinner every day the young Comrade Grisha Usievich—he fell in the civil war in 1919

—would come up for a half hour on his way from the emigrant's dining-room. For a time we had morning visits from a nephew of Zemlyatchka, who later became insane as a result of starvation. He was so tattered and spattered with mud that they refused to admit him to the Swiss libraries. He tried to see Ilyich before the latter left for the library, saying that he had to discuss certain matters of principle with him and got considerably on Ilyich's nerves.

We began leaving the house earlier in order to take a walk by the lake and have a chat before library time. Ilyich spoke of the book he was writing and of his various ideas.

Those of the Zurich group we met most frequently were Usievich and Kharitonov. I also remember "Uncle Vanya"—Avdeyev, a metal worker, Turkin, a worker from the Urals, and Boytsov, who later worked in the Central Bureau of Political Education (*Glavpolitprosviet*). I recall, too, a Bulgarian worker, whose name I have forgotten. Most of the comrades of our Zurich group worked in factories; they were all very busy and group meetings were comparatively rare. To make up for this, the members of the group had good connections with the workers of Zurich; they were closer to the life of the local workers than our groups in other Swiss cities (with the exception of Chaux-de-Fonds, where our group was even closer to the mass of workers).

At the head of the Swiss movement in Zurich was Fritz Platten; he was the secretary of the Party. He was an adherent of the Zimmerwald Left Group, was the son of a worker—a simple, ardent fellow who had much influence upon the masses. The editor of *Volksrecht*, Nobbs, also joined the Zimmerwald Lefts. The young emigrant workers—there

were many of them in Zurich—with Willi Muenzenberg at the head, were very active, supporting the
Lefts. All this brought us rather close to the Swiss
labour movement. Some comrades who had never
lived among the emigrés now think that Ilyich had
particular hopes of the Swiss movement and thought
that Switzerland might become almost the centre
of the coming social revolution.

This, of course, is not so. There was no strong
working class in Switzerland; it is mainly a country
of health resorts, a small country feeding on the
crumbs of the strong capitalist countries. The
workers of Switzerland are, on the whole, not very
revolutionary. Democracy, and the successful solu-
tion of the national question were not sufficient to
make Switzerland the hotbed of the social revolution.

This did not mean, of course, that it was not
necessary to conduct international propaganda in
Switzerland and to help revolutionise the Swiss
labour movement and the Party, for if Switzerland
were drawn into the war, the situation might have
changed quickly.

Ilyich delivered lectures to audiences of Swiss
workers, maintained close contact with Platten,
Nobbs and Muenzenberg. Our Zurich group and a
few Polish comrades (Comrade Bronsky was at that
time living in Zurich) undertook to arrange joint
meetings with the Swiss organisations in Zurich.
They began gathering in a small café, "Zum Adler,"
not far from our house. The first meeting was attended by about forty persons. Ilyich spoke on
current events and posed the problems very sharply.
Though the gathering consisted of internationalists,
the Swiss were quite embarrassed by the sharpness
with which Ilyich made his points. I remember the

speech of a representative of the Swiss youth to the effect that one cannot break through a stone wall with one's forehead. The fact remains that our meetings began to melt away, and to the fourth meeting only the Russians and the Poles came, and after exchanging some banter they went home.

During the first months of our stay in Zurich, Vladimir Ilyich worked mainly on his pamphlet on imperialism. He was very much absorbed in this work and copied numerous excerpts from the works he read. He was particularly interested in colonies; he had gathered a wealth of material and I remember how he put me to work translating from the English something about some African colonies. He narrated many interesting things. Later, when I re-read his *Imperialism* it seemed to me much drier than his stories had been. He studied the economic life of Europe, America, etc., as the saying goes, to a "t." But, of course, he was not only interested in the economic system, but also in the political forms that corresponded to that system and their influence on the masses. By June the pamphlet was completed. The second Zimmerwald Conference (the so-called Kienthal Conference) took place April 24th-30th, 1916. Eight months had elapsed since the first conference, eight months of ever-broadening imperialist war, yet the face of the Kienthal Conference was not so strikingly different from the first Zimmerwald Conference. The Zimmerwald left group had twelve instead of eight delegates, the resolutions of the conference marked a step forward. The conference defiantly condemned the International Socialist Bureau, adopting a resolution on peace which stated: "It is impossible to establish firm peace on the foundation of capitalist society; the conditions necessary for its realisation will be created by *Socialism*. By

N

abolishing capitalist private property and thereby abolishing the exploitation of the masses of the people by the propertied classes and national oppression, Socialism will also abolish the causes of war. For this reason, the struggle for a durable peace can only take the form of a struggle for the realisation of Socialism." Three German officers and thirty-two privates were executed in May for distributing this manifesto in the trenches. The German Government feared the revolutionisation of the masses more than anything else.

In its proposals to the Kienthal Conference, the Central Committee of the Russian Social-Democratic Labour Party called attention precisely to the necessity of revolutionising the masses. The proposals stated: "It is not enough that the Zimmerwald manifesto hints at revolution by saying that the workers must make sacrifices for their own cause, and not for another's cause. It is necessary to point out to the masses clearly and definitely the road they are to take. The masses must know where they are going and why. It is obvious that revolutionary mass action during the war, if successfully developed, can only lead to the transformation of the imperialist war into civil war for Socialism, and to conceal this from the masses is harmful. On the contrary, this aim must be pointed out clearly, no matter how difficult its attainment may seem to be when we are only at the beginning of the road. It is not enough to say what is stated in the Zimmerwald manifesto that 'the capitalists are lying when they speak of the defence of the Fatherland' in the present war and that in their revolutionary struggle the workers should not pay any attention to the war position of their country; it must be stated clearly what is only hinted at in the manifesto, that not only the

THE YEARS OF WAR TO FEBRUARY REVOLUTION 185

capitalists, but also the social-chauvinists and the
Kautskyites are lying when they concede that the
concept of defence of the fatherland is applicable to
the present imperialist war; that revolutionary
action in war-time is impossible without incurring
the danger of defeat for the home government and
that every defeat of the government in a reactionary
war facilitates revolution which alone can bring
about a lasting and democratic peace. Finally, it is
necessary to tell the masses that without their own
illegal organisations, created by themselves, and a
press free from military censorship, i.e. an illegal
press, it is impossible to render serious support to
the nascent revolutionary struggle, its development,
the criticism of its individual steps, the correction
of its errors and the systematic broadening and sharp-
ening of the struggle."

In this proposal of the Central Committee we find
a clear expression of the attitude of the Bolsheviks
and Ilyich to the masses; the masses must always be
told the whole truth, the unvarnished truth, without
fearing that the truth will frighten them away.
The Bolsheviks placed all their hopes in the masses
—the masses and only the masses will attain
Socialism.

In a letter to Shlyapnikov dated June 1st, I wrote:
"Gregory is very enthusiastic about Kienthal.
Of course, I can judge only by reports, but there
seems to have been too much rhetoric and no inner
unity, the kind of unity that would be a guarantee of
the solidity of the thing. It seems that the masses
are not yet 'pushing' as Badaich expressed it, except
perhaps, to some extent, the Germans."

The study of the economics of imperialism, the
analysis of the component parts of this "gear box,"
the grasp of the entire world-picture of imperialism

—this last stage of capitalism—heading for ruin—all this enabled Ilyich to present a number of political problems in a new way and to approach more profoundly the question as to the forms which the struggle for Socialism in general, and in Russia in particular, would assume. Ilyich wanted very much to think his ideas out to the end, to give them time to mature; so we decided to go to the mountains; and, moreover, it was necessary for us to go, for I could not shake off my illness. There was only one way of securing relief—the mountains. We went for six weeks to the Canton of St. Galeene, not far from Zurich, to the Chudivise rest-home amidst wild mountains, very high up and not far from the snow-peaks. The rest resort was quite inexpensive, $2\frac{1}{2}$ francs a day per person. It is true, it was a resort where they kept one on a milk diet. In the morning they served coffee with milk, bread and butter and cheese, but they gave us no sugar; for lunch—milk soup, something made of cheese-curds and milk; at four o'clock again coffee with milk and in the evening another milk meal. During the first days we positively howled against this milk-cure, then we began to supplement it by eating raspberries and blackberries which grew in the vicinity in great quantities. Our room was clean, with electric light, but without service; we had to tidy up the room ourselves and clean our own shoes. The latter function was assumed, emulating the Swiss, by Vladimir Ilyich, and every morning he would take my mountain shoes and his and go to the shed set aside for this purpose, exchanging pleasantries with other boot-blacks and displaying such zeal that once he knocked down a wicker-basket full of empty beer bottles, to the accompaniment of general laughter. The crowd was a democratic one. A rest-resort charging $2\frac{1}{2}$ francs a day per person is not patronised by "respectable" people. In some respect, this rest-resort resembled the French Bonbon, but the people were simpler, poorer, with a Swiss democratic veneer. In the evenings the proprietor's son played the accordian and the guests who came to rest danced for all they were worth, the stamping of the dancers resounding until eleven o'clock.

Chudivise was about eight kilometres from the station, communication was possible only by donkeys, the road was a narrow mountain path, everybody went on foot, and almost every morning about six o'clock a bell would ring, the public would gather to see the hikers off, and they would sing a farewell song about a cuckoo. Every verse ended with the words: "Good-bye, cuckoo." Vladimir Ilyich, who liked to sleep in the morning, would grumble and bury his head under the quilt. The crowd was extremely non-political. They did not even talk about the war. Among the visitors at the house was a soldier. His lungs were not particularly sturdy, and the authorities had sent him, at the state's expense, to take the cure at the "Milk" sanatorium. In Switzerland the military authorities take good care of the soldiers (Switzerland has a militia, not a permanent army). He was quite a nice fellow. Vladimir Ilyich hovered about him like a cat after lard, tried several times to engage him in a conversation about the predatory character of the war; the fellow would not contradict him, but was clearly not interested. It seemed that he was very little interested in political questions in general, certainly less than in his stay at *Chudivise*.

No one came to visit us, there were no Russians living in the place and we were detached from all affairs, roaming the mountains for days on end. In

Chudivise Ilyich did not work at all. During our walks in the mountains he spoke a good deal about the questions that occupied his mind at that time, about the rôle of democracy, about the positive and negative sides of Swiss democracy, always expressing the same thought in different words. Apparently these questions were engaging his attention a great deal.

We lived in the mountains during the latter half of July and the month of August. When we left, the inmates of the sanatorium gave us, too, a send-off by singing "Good-bye, cuckoo." As we were descending through a wood, Vladimir Ilyich suddenly noticed white mushrooms, and in spite of the fact that it was raining he began eagerly picking them, as if they had been so many Zimmerwald Lefts. We were drenched to the bone, but picked a sackful of mushrooms. Of course we missed the train and had to wait two hours at the station for the next one.

Upon arrival in Zurich we again took a room with the same people on Spiegelstrasse.

During our stay at Chudivise Vladimir Ilyich thought out from every angle his plan of work for the immediate future. The first thing of importance, particularly at that moment, was agreement on matters of theory, the establishment of a clear theoretical line. He had differences of opinion with Rosa Luxemburg, Radek, the Dutch, Bukharin, Piatakov and a little also with Kollontai. His sharpest differences were with Piatakov (P. Kievsky) who in August had written an article entitled "The Proletariat and the Right of Nations to Self-Determination." After reading the manuscript Vladimir Ilyich immediately sat down to write him an answer —a whole pamphlet, *A Caricature of Marxism and*

Imperialist Economism. The pamphlet was written in a very angry tone, and precisely for the reason that at that time Ilyich had already worked out a very clear, definite view of the relationship between economics and politics in the epoch of struggle for Socialism. The under-estimation of the political struggle in that epoch he characterised as imperialist economism. In this pamphlet Ilyich wrote: "Capitalism is victorious, *therefore* it is not necessary to think about political questions, this was the argument used by the old 'economists' in 1894-1901, who went so far as to repudiate the political struggle in Russia. Imperialism is victorious, *therefore* it is not necessary to think about questions of political democracy, is the argument of the modern 'imperialist economics.' "*

The rôle of democracy in the struggle for Socialism cannot be ignored. "Socialism is impossible without democracy in two respects,"—Vladimir Ilyich wrote in the same pamphlet—1. "the proletariat cannot accomplish the Socialist revolution if it is not prepared for it through the struggle for democracy; 2. victorious Socialism cannot maintain its victory and bring humanity to the time when the state will die out without the complete realisation of democracy."†

These words were soon fully justified by events in Russia. The February revolution and the subsequent struggle for democracy prepared the way for the revolution of October. The constant broadening and strengthening of the Soviets, of the Soviet system, reorganises democracy itself, constantly deepening the content of this concept.

In 1915-1916 Vladimir Ilyich had already thor-

* Lenin, *Collected Works*, Vol. XIX.
† *Ibid.*

oughly thought out the question of democracy, approaching the question from the standpoint of building Socialism. As early as November 1915, in replying to an article by Radek ("Parabellum") printed in the *Berner Tagewacht* in October 1915, Ilyich wrote:

"As to Comrade Parabellum, he, in the name of the Socialist revolution, scornfully rejects a consistently revolutionary programme in the realm of democracy. This is incorrect. The proletariat cannot become victor save through democracy, i.e. through introducing complete democracy and through combining with every step of its movement democratic demands formulated most vigorously, most decisively. It is senseless to *contrast* the Socialist revolution and the revolutionary struggle against capitalism with *one* of the questions of democracy, in this case the national question. On the contrary, we must combine the revolutionary struggle against capitalism with a revolutionary programme and revolutionary tactics relative to *all* democratic demands: a republic, a militia, officials elected by the people, equal rights for women, self-determination of nations, etc. While capitalism exists, all these demands are realisable only as an exception, and in incomplete, distorted form. Basing ourselves on democracy as it already exists, exposing its incompleteness under capitalism, we advocate the overthrow of capitalism, expropriation of the bourgeoisie as a necessary basis both for the abolition of the poverty of the masses and for a complete and manifold realisation of all democratic reforms. Some of those reforms will be started prior to the overthrow of the bourgeoisie, others in the process of the overthrow, still others after it has been accomplished.

* *Collected Works*, Vol. XIX.

The Socialist revolution is by no means a single battle; on the contrary, it is an epoch of a whole series of battles around *all* problems of economic and democratic reforms, which can be completed only by the expropriation of the bourgeoisie. It is for the sake of this final aim that we must formulate in a consistently revolutionary manner every one of our democractic demands. It is quite conceivable that the workers of a certain country may overthrow the bourgeoisie *before* even one fundamental democratic reform has been realised in full. It is entirely inconceivable, however, that the proletariat as an historical class will be able to defeat the bourgeoisie if it is not prepared for this task by being educated in the spirit of the most consistent and determined revolutionary democracy."*

I quote such long passages because they very clearly express the ideas which left an imprint on his later utterances. Most of his articles dealing with the questions of the rôle of democracy in the struggle for Socialism were published much later; the article against "Parabellum"—in 1927, the pamphlet, *A Caricature of Marxism*, in 1924. They are little known because they were published in magazines with not very large circulations; yet without having read these articles one cannot understand the heat shown by Vladimir Ilyich in his arguments on the right of nations to self-determination. This heat becomes understandable when the matter is considered in connection with Ilyich's general estimation of democracy. It must be borne in mind that Ilyich regarded the attitude one took toward the question of self-determination as a test of one's ability to approach correctly democratic demands in general. All the disputes along this line with Rosa Luxem-

* Lenin, *Collected Works*, Vol. XVIII, p. 368.

burg, with Radek, the Dutch and Kievsky, as well as with other comrades, were conducted from just this point of view. In the pamphlet against Kievsky he wrote: "All nations will come to Socialism, this is inevitable, but they will not all reach it in the same way; every nation will introduce certain special features into this or that form of democracy, this or that variety of the dictatorship of the proletariat, this or that tempo of the Socialist transformations of the various sides of social life. There is nothing that is theoretically more paltry and practically more ridiculous than to picture, 'in the name of historical materialism,' a future painted, in this respect, in the same drab colour; this would be a mere Suzdal daub."

The building of Socialism is not only economic building. Economics is only the base of Socialist construction, its foundation, its premise; the crux of Socialist construction lies in the rebuilding of the entire social fabric, a rebuilding on the basis of Socialist revolutionary democracy.

This, perhaps, is what most divided Lenin and Trotsky. Trotsky did not understand the democratic spirit, the democratic principles of Socialist construction, the process of reorganising the entire mode of life of the masses. Also at that time, in 1916, the later differences between Ilyich and Bukharin already existed in embryo. At the end of August Bukharin wrote an article in the *Jugend-Internationale* No. 6, signed "Nota-Bene," which showed that he under-estimated the rôle of the state, under-estimated the rôle of the dictatorship of the proletariat. In a note in the *Jugend-Internationale* Ilyich pointed out this error of Bukharin's. The dictatorship of the proletariat, which ensures the leading rôle of the proletariat in the reconstruction of the entire social fabric—this is what particularly interested Vladimir Ilyich in the latter half of 1916.

Democratic demands are included in the minimum programme—and in the first letter he wrote to Shlyapnikov after returning from Chudivise, Ilyich scolds Bazarov for an article in *Letopisi* in which the latter advocated the abolition of the minimum programme. He argued with Bukharin who underestimated the rôle of the state, the rôle of the dictatorship of the proletariat, etc. He was indignant with Kievsky because the latter did not understand the leading rôle of the proletariat. "Don't look with disdain upon the harmony of theoretical opinion; honestly, it is needed in work during these difficult times."

Vladimir Ilyich began diligently re-reading all that had been written by Marx and Engels on the state, and took extracts from their works. This equipped him with a particularly profound understanding of the nature of the coming revolution, and prepared him most thoroughly for the understanding of the concrete tasks of that revolution.

On November 30th a conference of the Swiss Lefts took place on the attitude toward the war. A. Schmidt from Winterthur spoke of the necessity of taking advantage of the democratic system in Switzerland for anti-militarist purposes. Next day Lenin wrote a letter to A. Schmidt suggesting that a referendum be taken on the question, formulated in the following manner: for the expropriation of the large capitalist enterprises in industry and agriculture as the *only way* toward the complete abolition of militarism, or against expropriation.

"In this case we will in our practical politics say the same thing,"—Ilyich wrote to Schmidt, "that in theory we recognise that the complete abolition of militarism is conceivable only in conjunction with the abolition of capitalism." In a letter written in December 1916 and published only fifteen years later, Lenin wrote on this question: "Perhaps you think that I am so naïve as to believe that it is possible to solve such questions as the question about the Socialist revolution 'by means of persuasion?' No; I only wish to give an *illustration*, and then only of one *part of the question*, *viz.*, what *change* must take place in the entire propaganda of the Party if we want to take up a really serious attitude on the question of *rejecting the defence of the fatherland*! This is *only* an illustration to *only* a part of the question—I do not claim any more." Questions of a dialectical approach to the events of that period also occupied Ilyich. He simply clutched at the following sentence in Engels' criticism of the draft of the "Erfurt programme": "Such a policy can in the end only lead the Party on to the wrong road. General, abstract political questions are put in the foreground and thus obscure immediate concrete questions which will automatically come up on the order of the day at the very first outbreak of big events, in the first political crisis." Having copied this passage Ilyich wrote in very large letters, putting the words in double parentheses: "((The abstract in the foreground, the concrete obscured!!)) Nota Bene! Excellent! That's the main thing! N.B."

"Marxian dialectics demands a concrete analysis of every particular historical situation," wrote Vladimir Ilyich in his review of the pamphlet by Junius. He particularly strove during that period to consider all things in all their connections and interrelations. From this standpoint he approached both the question of democracy and of the right of nations to self-determination.

In the autumn of 1916 and at the beginning of 1917 Ilyich steeped himself in theoretical work. He tried to utilise all the time the library was open. He got there exactly at 9 o'clock, stayed until 12, came home exactly at 10 minutes past 12 (the library was closed from 12 to 1), after lunch he returned to the library and stayed there until 6 o'clock. It was not very convenient to work at home. Although we had a light room, the windows faced a yard from which came an intolerable stench, for a sausage factory adjoined the yard. We opened the window only late at night. On Thursdays, after lunch, when the library was closed, we went to the Zurichberg mountain. On his way from the library Ilyich usually bought two bars of nut chocolate, in blue wrappers, at 15 centimes a piece, and after lunch we took the chocolate and some books and went to the mountain. We had a favourite spot there in the very thick of the woods, where there was no crowd. Ilyich would lie there on the grass and read diligently.

At that time we instituted a doubly rigid economy in our personal life. Ilyich searched everywhere for something to earn—he wrote about it to Granat, to Gorky, to relatives and once even developed a fantastic plan to publish a "pedagogical encyclopedia," on which I was to work. At that time I did considerable work studying pedagogical questions and familiarising myself with the practical side of the schools in Zurich. Ilyich got so enthusiastic about this fantastic plan that he wrote something to the effect that care must be taken lest someone steal this idea.

The prospect of earning something by writing was rather poor, and I therefore decided to look for work in Zurich. In Zurich there was the Bureau of the Political Emigrant Relief organisations, at the head of which was Felix Yakovlevich Kon. I became the secretary of the Bureau and helped Felix Yakovlevich in his work.

It is true that the income from this was semi-mythical, but the work had to be done. Assistance had to be given to comrades to find work, to organise various undertakings and to organise medical assistance. Funds were very low at that time and there were more projects than real assistance. I remember a plan was proposed to establish a sanatorium on a self-paying basis; the Swiss have such sanatoria. The patients work several hours a day at gardening or making cane chairs in the open air and this helps to reduce the cost of their maintenance. The percentage of consumptives among the political emigrants was very large.

So we lived in Zurich, unhurriedly and quietly, while the situation became much more revolutionary. Along with his work in the realm of theory Ilyich considered it of the greatest importance to work out a correct tactical line. He thought that the time was ripe for a split on an international scale, that it was necessary to break with the Second International, with the International Socialist Bureau, to break forever with Kautsky and Co., to begin with the forces of the Zimmerwald Lefts to build a Third International. In Russia it was necessary at once to break with Tcheidze, Skovelev and the followers of the Organisation Committee,* with those who, like Trotsky, did not understand that this was no time for reconciliation and talk about unity. It was necessary to conduct a revolutionary struggle for Socialism and to expose ruthlessly the opportunists whose words did not match their deeds, who in

* The leading body of the Mensheviks.—Ed.

reality were serving the bourgeoisie and betraying the cause of the proletariat. Never, I think, was Vladimir Ilyich in a more irreconcilable mood than during the last months of 1916 and the early months of 1917. He was profoundly convinced that the revolution was approaching.

1917

Before the October Revolution

On January 22nd, 1917, Vladimir Ilyich delivered a lecture on the 1905 Revolution at a youth meeting organised in the Zurich Peoples' House. At the time there were many young people of revolutionary tendencies in Zurich from other countries—Germany, Italy, etc., who did not want to participate in the imperialist war. Vladimir Ilyich wanted to convey to these young people as fully as possible the experience of the revolutionary struggle of the workers, to show them the significance of the Moscow uprising. He considered the 1905 Revolution to be a prologue to the coming European revolution. "Undoubtedly," he said, "this coming revolution can only be a proletarian revolution, and in the profounder sense of this word: a proletarian, Socialist revolution even in its content. This coming revolution will show to an even greater degree on the one hand that only stern battles, only civil wars, can free humanity from the yoke of capital; on the other hand that only the class-conscious proletarians can and will come forth in the rôle of leaders of the vast majority of exploited." Ilyich did not for one minute doubt that such were the prospects. But naturally, he could not know how soon this coming revolution would take place. "We of the older generation may not live to see the decisive battles of this coming revolution," he said sadly, in concluding his lecture.*

* *The Revolution of 1905.* Little Lenin Library, No. 6.—Ed.

And yet Ilyich thought of and worked only for this coming revolution. But once, after dinner, when Ilyich was getting ready to leave for the library, and I had finished with the dishes, Bronsky ran in with the announcement, "Haven't you heard the news? There is a revolution in Russia!"—and told us what was written in the special editions of the newspapers that were issued. When Bronsky left, we went to the lake, where on the shore all the newspapers were hung up as soon as they came out.

We read the telegrams over several times. There really was a revolution in Russia. Ilyich's mind worked intensely. I do not remember how the rest of the day and the evening passed. Next day the second series of government telegrams dealing with the February revolution were received and Ilyich was already writing to Kollontai in Stockholm. "*Never again* along the lines of the Second International! *Never again* with Kautsky! By all means a *more revolutionary* programme and more revolutionary tactics." And further, "revolutionary propaganda, as heretofore, agitation and struggle for an *international* proletarian revolution and for the seizure of power by the 'Soviets of Workers' Deputies' (but not by the Cadet fakers)."*

Ilyich immediately took a clear, uncompromising line, but he had not yet grasped the scope of the revolution. Measuring it by that of the 1905 Revolution, he said that the most important task at that moment was to combine legal and illegal work.

Next day, in answer to Kollontai's telegram asking for instructions, he wrote differently, more concretely. He did not write of the seizure of power by the Soviets of Workers' Deputies as a perspective, but urged that concrete measures be taken to pre-

* Lenin, *Collected Works*, Vol. XX, Book I, p. 20.

O

pare for the seizure of power, for arming the masses, for the fight for bread, peace and freedom. "Spread out! Rouse new sections! Awaken fresh initiative, form new organisations in every layer and *prove* to them that *peace* can come only with the armed Soviet of Workers' Deputies in power."* Together with Zinoviev, Ilyich set out to work on theses on the February revolution.

From the moment news of the February revolution came, Ilyich burned with eagerness to go to Russia.

England and France would not for the world have allowed the Bolsheviks to pass through to Russia. This was clear to Ilyich—"we fear," he wrote to Kollontai—"we will not succeed in leaving this cursed Switzerland very soon." And taking this into consideration, he, in his letters of March 16th and 17th, made arrangements with Kollontai how best to re-establish contacts with Petrograd.

As there was no legal way it was necessary to travel illegally. But how? From the moment the news of the revolution came, Ilyich did not sleep, and at night all sorts of incredible plans were made. We could travel by airplane. But such things could be thought of only in the semi-delirium of the night. One had only to formulate it vocally to realise the utter impracticability of such a plan. A passport of a foreigner from a neutral country would have had to be obtained, a Swedish passport would be best as a Swede arouses less suspicion. A Swedish passport could have been obtained through the aid of the Swedish comrades, but there was the further obstacle of our not knowing the Swedish language. Perhaps only a little Swedish would do. But it would be so easy to give one's self away. "You will fall asleep and see Mensheviks in your dreams and you

* Lenin, *Collected Works*, Vol. XX, Book I, p. 22.

will start swearing, and shout, scoundrels, scoundrels! and give the whole conspiracy away," I said to him teasingly.

Still, Ilyich inquired of Ganetsky as to whether there was some way in which he could be smuggled through Germany.

On March 18th, the anniversary of the Paris Commune, Ilyich went to Chaux-de-Fonds, a large Swiss workers' centre. Ilyich was very glad to go. A young comrade named Abramovich who worked at a factory, and was active in the Swiss labour movement, lived there. Ilyich had been thinking about the Paris Commune, of how to make use of its experience in the nascent Russian revolutionary movement, and of how to avoid its errors, and so his lecture went off very well, and he was pleased with it himself. The lecture produced a profound impression on our comrades, but the Swiss thought it somewhat visionary—even the centres of the Swiss working-class movement understood very dimly the events that were taking place in Russia.

On March 19th there was a meeting of the Russian political emigré groups in Switzerland, which adhered to the international position, to discuss ways and means of getting back to Russia. Martov presented a plan to obtain permits for emigrants to pass through Germany in exchange for German and Austrian prisoners of war interned in Russia. But no one wanted to go that way, except Lenin, who snatched at this plan. The plan had to be carried out carefully, and it was thought that it would be best for the Swiss government to take the initiative in raising the matter. Grimm was commissioned to open negotiations with the Swiss government, but nothing came of it; the telegrams that were sent to Russia were not answered. Ilyich was in great distress. "What a torment it is for all of us to sit here at such a time," he wrote to Ganetsky in Stockholm. But he had already put himself under complete self-control.

On March 18th, *Pravda* began to be issued in Petrograd and on the 20th Ilyich started sending his "Letters from Afar" to the paper. There were five letters (*The First Stage of the First Revolution, The New Government and the Proletariat, On Proletarian Militia, How to Secure Peace, Problems of Revolutionary Proletarian Organisation of the State*). Only the first letter had been published when Lenin finally arrived in Petrograd, three were lying in the editor's office and the fifth had not even been sent to *Pravda*, as Lenin had only started writing it on the eve of his departure to Russia.

These letters reflect clearly Ilyich's thoughts just before his departure. I particularly remember what he then said about the militia. The third "Letter from Afar," *On Proletarian Militia* is devoted to this question. It was published only after Lenin's death in 1924. In it Ilyich presents his ideas on the proletarian state. Those who want thoroughly to understand Lenin's book, *State and Revolution*, must read this "Letter from Afar." The whole article treats the subject with extraordinary concreteness. Ilyich speaks of a new type of militia created by the general arming of citizens, consisting of all adults of both sexes. In addition to its military duties, this militia must secure the proper and speedy distribution of bread and other provisions, must act as sanitary inspectors, see that every family has bread, every child a bottle of good milk and that no adult in a rich family dare to take extra milk until all children are supplied, that the palaces and rich homes do not remain unoccupied, but that they shelter the homeless and destitute.

"What other organisation except a universal people's militia with women participating on an equal footing with the men can effect these measures?" Ilyich wrote.

"Such measures *do not yet* constitute Socialism. They deal with distribution of articles of consumption, not with the reorganisation of production. Theoretical classification doesn't matter now. It would indeed be a grave error if we tried now to fit the complex, urgent, rapidly unfolding practical tasks of the revolution into the procrustean bed of a narrowly conceived 'theory,' instead of regarding theory first of all and above all as a *guide to action*."* The proletarian militia should actually educate the masses to take part in all state affairs. "Such a militia would draw the youngsters into political life, training them not only by word, but by deed and *work*."† "Our immediate problem is organisation, not in the sense of effecting ordinary organisation by ordinary methods, but in the sense of drawing large masses of the oppressed classes in unheard of numbers into the organisation, and of embodying in this organisation military, state and national economic problems."‡ Re-reading this letter after a lapse of many years, I can picture him as if he were before me now: his extraordinary sober-mindedness, his clear appreciation of the necessity of an irreconcilable armed struggle, and of the fact that no concessions or vacillation could be permitted at that moment; and on the other hand, his close attention to the mass movement, to the organisation of the broad masses in a new way, to their concrete needs, and to the immediate improvement of their conditions. Ilyich spoke of all these matters in the winter

* Lenin, *Collected Works*, Volume XX, Book I, p. 57.
† *Ibid.*, p. 53. ‡ *Ibid.*, p. 55.

of 1916-17 and especially on the eve of the February revolution.

The negotiations dragged on. The Provisional government evidently did not want to allow the internationalists to enter Russia; news came from Russia of vacillation among the comrades. All this made it imperative to hasten our departure. Ilyich sent a telegram to Ganetsky who received it only on March 25th, in which he said: "We do not understand the delay. The Mensheviks want the sanction of the Soviet of Workers' Deputies. Send someone immediately to Finland or Petrograd to come to terms with Chkheidze. Opinion of Belenin desirable." By Belenin was meant the Bureau of the Central Committee. When Kollontai arrived in Russia on March 18th she related how matters stood with Ilyich's coming; letters were received from Ganetsky. The Bureau of the Central Committee sent a message through Ganetsky saying, "Ulyanov must come immediately." Ganetsky re-telegraphed this message to Lenin. Vladimir Ilyich insisted that negotiations be opened through Fritz Platten, the Swiss Socialist-internationalist. Platten concluded a precise written agreement with the German ambassador in Switzerland. The main points of this agreement were: 1. All the emigrants regardless of their opinions on the war to be allowed to go; 2. No one to be allowed to enter the railway car in which the emigrants were travelling without Platten's permission. No inspection of passports or baggage; 3. The travellers undertake to agitate in Russia for the exchange of a number of Austro-German prisoners interned in Russia equal to the number of emigrants allowed to travel by this agreement. Ilyich energetically began to prepare for the journey, and wrote letters to Berne, Geneva and a

number of comrades. The *Vperyod*-ists with whom
Ilyich was negotiating refused to go. Karl and
Kasparov, two close comrades, had to remain, they
were very sick and dying in Davos. Ilyich wrote
them a farewell greeting.

Ilyich wrote an article for the Zurich paper *Volksrecht*, entitled "The Tasks of the Russian Social-Democratic Labour Party in the Russian Revolution,"*
and also a "Farewell Letter to the Swiss Workers,"
which ended with the words "Long live the proletarian revolution that is *beginning* in Europe!"† Ilyich
also addressed a letter to "Comrades Languishing in
Captivity," Russian prisoners of war, in which he
told them about the revolution and of the coming
struggle. We had to write to them. While still in
Berne, a rather considerable correspondence was
started with Russian prisoners of war languishing
in German camps. Of course, we could not help
them much as far as material comforts were concerned, but we helped all we could by writing letters
to them and sending them literature. A number
of close connections were made, and after our departure from Berne the Safarovs continued this
work. We sent these prisoners of war illegal literature, Kollontai's pamphlet on war which had a very
good effect, and a number of leaflets.

A few months before we left, two prisoners of war,
one a Voronezh peasant named Michaelev, and the
other an Odessa worker, arrived at Zurich and
came to our group. They had escaped from Germany by swimming across Lake Boden. Ilyich discussed many things with them. Michaelev's stories
of his captivity were especially interesting. He told
us that at first the Ukrainian prisoners were sent to

* Lenin, *Collected Works*, Vol. XX, Book I, p. 77.
† *Ibid.*, pp. 82-88

Galicia, that pro-Ukrainian agitation against Russia was carried on among them, that he was sent to Germany where he was compelled to work on wealthy peasant farms. "How wonderfully they manage everything, not a crust is wasted," exclaimed Michaelev. Although his people were old believers and his grandfather and grandmother had therefore forbidden him to learn to read and write (as literacy was the stamp of the devil), he learned to read and write in Germany. His grandmother and grandfather sent him millet and fat while he was in Germany and the Germans looked on with amazement as he cooked and ate millet gruel. Michaelev had intended to take university extension courses and resented the fact that none were given in Zurich. He was interned and put to work as a labourer. He was very much surprised at how cowed the Swiss workers were. "I went," he said, "to the office to draw my pay and saw Swiss workers crouched against the wall peeping in through the window, not daring to enter the office. What a subdued people. I went up, opened the door and walked into the office. I went to get money for my work!" Ilyich was very interested in this peasant from Central Russia, who had just learned to read and write and yet expressed surprise at the subjection of the Swiss workers. Michaelev also told us that one day a Russian priest visited the prisoners' camp but that the soldiers refused to listen to him and began to shout and swear. One of the prisoners went over to the priest, kissed his hand and said, "Go away, little father, this is no place for you." Michaelev and his comrades asked us to take them to Russia with us, but we did not know what would happen to us—we might all be arrested again. After our departure, Michaelev crossed over to France, first lived in

Paris, then worked in a tractor plant and then went
to Eastern France, where there were many Polish
emigrants. In 1918 (or 1919, I don't remember
exactly) Michaelev returned to Russia and met
Ilyich. He related how he and several other prisoners
of war who had escaped from Germany were called
to the Russian Embassy, where it was suggested to
them that they sign a manifesto calling for the continuation of the war to a victorious end. Though
important officials decorated with orders spoke to
the soldiers, they refused to sign the manifesto. "I
got up and said that the war must end and left. The
others also quietly walked out," he said. He also
told of the anti-war agitation which was carried on
by the youth in the small French town where he
lived. Michaelev now did not in the least resemble
the Voronezh peasant we first met: he wore a French
cap, khaki-coloured puttees, and his face was clean
shaven. Ilyich obtained work for him in a factory.
But all his thoughts were of his native village, which
had passed from hand to hand, from the reds to the
whites and back again. The whole centre of the village
he came from had been burned down by the whites,
but his house had escaped destruction and his grandmother and grandfather were still alive. Michaelev
came to my office at the Central Board of Political
Education and told me all this and that he was preparing to go home. "Why aren't you on the way?" I
asked. "I am waiting until my beard grows back,
grandma and grandpa will die of grief if they see me
shaved." A little while ago I received a letter from
him. He is working on the railroad in Central Asia;
he wrote that on Lenin Memorial Day he spoke at
a meeting at a workers' club and related how, in 1917,
he saw Ilyich in Zurich and told them of our life
abroad. Everybody listened with interest but they

doubted the truth of the story and so Michaelev asked me to vouch for the fact that he had visited Ilyich in Zurich.

Michaelev was a piece of real life, and so also were the letters sent to our Prisoners of War Aid Committee.

Ilyich could not leave for Russia without writing to them about the things that interested him most at the time.

The Kammerers, of whom we had rented a room, had taken an apartment in a new house. In the new, clean and light apartment, we were allotted a large, comfortable room, but we only lived there a few days.

When the letter came from Berne informing us that Platten's negotiations had come to a successful conclusion and that only the protocol had to be signed, and we could move on to Russia, Ilyich jumped up and said: "We will take the first train." The train was due to leave within two hours. We had just these two hours to liquidate our entire "household," settle accounts with the landlady, return the books to the library, pack up and so on. "Go yourself, I will leave to-morrow," I said. But Ilyich insisted, "No, we will go together." In the two hours everything was done: books packed, letters destroyed, the necessary clothing and things chosen, and all affairs settled, and we caught the first train to Berne. We need not have hurried, however, for it was Easter and for that reason the train was late in starting.

The comrades going to Russia met in the Berne People's House; the Zinovievs, Usyevich, Inessa Armand, the Safarovs, Olga Ravich, Abramovich from Chaux-de-Fonds, Grebelskaya, Haritonov, Linde, Rosenbloom, Boytsov, Mikha Tskhakay, the Marienhoffs, Sokolnikov, Radek under the guise of a Russian and others. Altogether, thirty people travelled, without counting curly-headed Robert, the four-year-old son of a member of the Bund.

Fritz Platten accompanied us.

The defensists raised a hullabaloo about the Bolsheviks travelling through Germany. Of course, in giving us permission to travel, the German government was under the impression that revolution was a terrible disaster for a country and thought that by allowing emigré-internationalists to pass through to their native country they would help to spread this "disaster" in Russia. The Bolsheviks were very little concerned with what the bourgeois German government thought. They considered it their duty to spread revolutionary propaganda in Russia and set as the aim of their activities the achievement of the victorious proletarian revolution. They knew that the defensists would throw mud at them, but they knew also that the masses would finally follow their lead. On March 27th the Bolsheviks alone risked the route through Germany, but a month later more than two hundred emigrants, including Martov and other Mensheviks, followed the same route.

In boarding the train, no questions were asked about the baggage and passports. Ilyich kept entirely to himself, his thoughts were in Russia. En route, the conversation was mainly trivial, Robert's cheerful voice could be heard through the whole car. He particularly liked Sokolnikov and did not want to talk to the women. The Germans tried to show us that they had plenty of everything, the cook prepared exceptionally big meals, to which our emigrant fraternity were not greatly accustomed. Through the car window we noticed a surprising absence of adult men; some women, boys and girls in their teens and children could be seen at the stations, on the fields and city streets. I was often reminded of this picture during the first days in Petrograd where I was surprised that the street cars were so crowded with soldiers.

On arrival in Berlin our train was shunted on to a siding. Near Berlin several German Social-Democrats entered a special compartment. No one of our people spoke to them, except Robert, who looked into their compartment and asked in French "What does the conductor do?" I do not know whether the Germans answered Robert, but I do know that they were not able to put the questions they wanted to go to the Bolsheviks. On March 31st we arrived in Sweden. At Stockholm we were met by the Swedish Social-Democratic deputies, Lindhagen, Carlson, Ström, Ture Nerman and others. A red flag was hung up in the waiting-room and a meeting was held. I remember little of Stockholm; all thoughts were in Russia. The Russian Provisional Government did not permit Fritz Platten and Radek to enter Russia but did not dare to stop the Bolsheviks. From Sweden we crossed to Finland in small Finnish sledges. Everything was already familiar and dear to us—the wretched third-class cars, the Russian soldiers. It was terribly good. It was not long before Robert was in the arms of an elderly soldier, clasping his neck with his small arms, chattering to him in French and eating Easter cheese with which the soldier fed him. Our people were huddled against the windows. The station platforms we passed were crowded with soldiers. Usyevich leaned out of the window and shouted: "Long live the world revolution!" The soldiers looked at him puzzled. A pale-faced lieutenant passed us a few times, and when Ilyich and I went into a nearby empty car, he sat

down beside Ilyich and spoke to him. The lieutenant was a defensist, and they started an argument.
Ilyich put his point of view—he, too, was dreadfully
pale. Soldiers began squeezing into the car until
there was no room to move. The soldiers stood on
the benches so as the better to see and hear the one
who was speaking so convincingly against the predatory war. And as the minutes passed they became
more attentive and their faces became more tense.

Maria Ilyinishna, Shlyapnikov, Stahl and other
comrades and women workers met us at Beloostrov.
Stahl urged me to say a few words of greeting to the
women workers, but all words had left me, I could
say nothing. Ilyich asked the comrades who sat
with us if we would be arrested on our arrival; they
smiled. Soon we arrived in Petrograd.

The Petrograd masses, workers, soldiers and sailors
came to meet their leader. Among the many close
comrades there, was Churgurin—a student at the
Longjumeau school, his face wet with tears, wearing
a wide red sash across his shoulder. There was a
sea of people all around.

Those who have not lived through the revolution
cannot imagine its grand, solemn beauty. Red
banners, a guard of honour of Kronstadt sailors,
searchlights from the Fortress of Peter and Paul
illuminating the road from the Finland station to the
Kshesinsky Mansion,* armoured cars, a chain of
working men and women guarding the road.

Chkheidze and Skobelev met us at the Finland
station as the official representatives of the Petrograd
Soviet of Workers' and Soldiers' Deputies. The
comrades led Ilyich to the tsar's rest-room where

* The former residence of the Tsar's mistress, the ballet dancer,
Kshesinskaya. The mansion became the headquarters of the
Bolshevik Party.—Ed.

Chkheidze and Skobelev were. When Ilyich came
out on the platform a captain came to him and,
standing at attention, reported something. Ilyich,
a little taken aback with surprise, saluted. Ilyich
and all our emigrant fraternity were led past a guard
of honour which was on the platform. Ilyich stood
on an armoured car, the rest were seated in automo-
biles and thus we drove to Kshesinsky Mansion.
"Long live the Socialist world revolution!" Ilyich
called out to the huge crowd of many thousands
surrounding us.

Ilyich sensed the beginning of this revolution in
every fibre of his body.

We arrived at the Kshesinsky Mansion where the
Central Committee and the Petrograd Committee
of the Party then had their headquarters. The Petrograd comrades had arranged a comradely tea and
wanted to organise speeches of welcome, but Ilyich
turned the conversation to what interested him
most, the tactics that had to be pursued. A huge
crowd of workers and soldiers surrounded the house.
Ilyich had to go out on the balcony and make a
speech. The impressions of the meeting, of the up-
heaval of revolutionary elements put everything else
into the shade.

We then went home to our people, to Anna
Ilyinishna and Mark Timofeyevich. They lived on
Shirokaya Street, on the Petrograd Side, and Maria
Ilyinishna lived with them. We were given a separate
room. In honour of our arrival, Gora, Anna Ilyini-
shna's foster son, hung over our beds the slogan,
"Workers of the World Unite." I hardly spoke to
Ilyich that night—there were really no words to
express the experience, everything was understood
without words.

Times were such that not a minute could be wasted.

Ilyich had not yet got up when a comrade came for
him. He went with Zinoviev to the Executive Committee of the Petrograd Soviet to report on the
journey through Germany. From there he went to
a conference of Bolsheviks—of the members of the
All-Russian Conference of Soviets of Workers' and
Soldiers' Deputies which was in session somewhere
on an upper floor of the Taurida Palace. In ten
theses Lenin expressed his opinion on what had to
be done. In these theses he gave his appraisal of the
situation, clearly and definitely laid down the aims
for which it was necessary to strive, and the road
that must be followed to reach them. For the first
few minutes our people were taken aback. It seemed
to many that Lenin presented the question too
bluntly, that it was still early to speak of Socialist
revolution.

A meeting of Mensheviks was in progress on the
floor below. A comrade came from there and insisted that Ilyich present the same report at a joint
meeting of Menshevik and Bolshevik delegates. At
the Bolshevik meeting it was decided that Ilyich
repeat the report at a general meeting of all Social-
Democrats. Ilyich did so. The joint meeting took
place downstairs in the large hall of the Taurida
Palace. I remember the first thing that caught my
eye was that Goldenberg (Meshkovsky) was in the
Presidium. In the 1905 revolution he was a strong
Bolshevik, one of the very closest comrades in the
struggle. Now he followed Plekhanov and had become a defensist.* Lenin spoke for about two hours.
Goldenberg was his opponent. He criticised Lenin
very sharply and said that Lenin had raised the
banner of civil war in the revolutionary democratic
midst. How far we had drifted apart was apparent.

* Later on Goldenberg rejoined the Bolshevik Party.—Ed.

I still remember Kollontai's fervent speech in defence of Lenin's theses.

In his newspaper *Edinstvo* (*Unity*), Plekhanov described Lenin's theses as "delirium."

Three days later, on April 7th, Lenin's theses were printed in *Pravda*. On the following day there was an article by Kamenev in *Pravda* entitled "Our Disagreements," in which he dissociated himself from Lenin's theses and stated that they were the expression of Lenin's private opinion, that they were not advocated either by *Pravda* or by the Bureau of the Central Committee. The Bolshevik delegates, at the meeting at which the theses were presented did not accept them, but accepted those of the Bureau of the Central Committee. Kamenev declared that *Pravda* maintained its old positions.

A struggle inside the Bolshevik organisation began, but it did not last long. In a week a general city conference of the Bolsheviks of Petrograd was held at which Ilyich's point of view triumphed. The conference continued eight days (April 14th-22nd), during which time a number of important events took place which proved how much in the right Lenin was.

On April 7th—the day Lenin's theses appeared in print—the Executive Committee of the Petrograd Soviet voted for the issue of a "Liberty Loan."

The bourgeois and defensist press started a furious campaign against Lenin and the Bolsheviks. Kamenev's statement was ignored. Everybody knew that Lenin's point of view would prevail in the ranks of the Bolshevik organisation. The campaign against Lenin served to popularise his theses. Lenin called the war an imperialist war of plunder and all saw that he was in earnest about peace. This roused the sailors and soldiers, it roused those for whom

the war was a question of life or death. On April
10th Lenin addressed the men of the Izmailovsky
regiment; on the 15th the *Soldatskaya Pravda* (*Soldiers'
Truth*) came out, and on the 16th the Petrograd
soldiers and sailors organised a demonstration to
protest against the campaign against Lenin and the
Bolsheviks.

On April 18th* (May 1st) grand May Day demonstrations took place throughout Russia, such as
had never been seen before.

On April 18th, Milyukov, Minister of Foreign
Affairs, issued a statement in the name of the
Provisional government, to the effect that it would
continue the war to a victorious conclusion and that
it would remain loyal to all obligations to the Allies.
What did the Bolsheviks do? They exposed what
these obligations were in their press—they pointed
out that the Provisional government had pledged
itself to carry out the obligations that were entered
into by the government of Nicholas II and the whole
tsarist gang. They pointed out that they were
obligations to the bourgeoisie.

When this became clear to the masses, they came
out on the streets. On April 21st they organised a
demonstration on the Nevsky. The supporters of
the Provisional government also organised a demonstration on the Nevsky.

These events united the Bolsheviks. The Bolshevik
organisation in Petrograd passed a resolution in
keeping with Lenin's views.

On April 21st and 22nd the Central Committee
passed a resolution which clearly pointed out the
need for exposing the Provisional government, condemned the conciliatory tactics of the Pretrograd

* The dates given in the text are according to the Russian old
style calendar.—Ed.

P

Soviet, called for a re-election of workers' and soldiers' deputies, called for the strengthening of the Soviets, appealed for a broad explanatory work and at the same time pointed out that attempts to overthrow the Provisional government immediately would be premature.

The All-Russian Conference opened on April 24th, three weeks after Lenin's theses had gained publicity and the Bolsheviks had achieved unity.

After our arrival in Petrograd, I saw little of Ilyich. He was working at the Central Committee, and in *Pravda*, and attending meetings. I worked at the Secretariat of the Central Committee in the Kshesinsky Mansion, but the work could not be compared with the Secretariat work abroad, or with that of 1905-07 when I had to carry on rather important work independently under Ilyich's directions. Stasova was the secretary; she was assisted by technical workers. I talked to the workers who came there. Still, I knew little of the local work. The Central Committee members came there frequently, Sverdlov most often of all. No special duties were assigned to me and the absence of definite work bored me. I greedily absorbed the life around me. The streets at that time presented an interesting sight; everywhere groups gathered, heatedly discussing the political situation and all the events that occurred. I used to mingle with the crowd and listen. Once I walked three hours from Shirokaya Street to the Kshesinsky Mansion, so interesting were these meetings. There was a courtyard opposite our house from which excited arguments could be heard when we opened the window at night. A soldier sat there always with someone—the cook, the maids from the neighbouring houses, or some youth. At one o'clock in the morning disjointed words could be

heard such as: Bolsheviks, Mensheviks. . . . At three
o'clock: Milyukov, Bolsheviks. . . . At five o'clock the
same; politics and meetings. The white nights of
Petrograd are now always associated in my mind
with these nightly gatherings.

I had to meet many people at the Secretariat of
the Central Committee; the Petrograd Committee,
the military organisation and *Soldatskaya Pravda*, all
were located at Kshesinsky Mansion. Sometimes I
attended the meetings of the Petrograd Committee
where I got to know the people more closely and
followed the committee's work. The children and
young workers also interested me very much. Children were taken up with the movement. Among
them were supporters of different trends—Bolsheviks,
Mensheviks, Socialist-Revolutionaries and anarchists. At first there were about fifty thousand youths
in the organisation, but at that time the movement
was left pretty much to itself. I carried on some work
among them. These young workers presented a
striking contrast to the older groups of the middle
school. These latter often approached the Kshesinsky Mansion in a crowd hurling abuse at the
Bolsheviks. It was apparent that they were put up
to it by someone.

Soon after our arrival—I do not remember the
exact date—I attended a teachers' congress. There
was a huge crowd: the teachers were completely
under the influence of the Socialist-Revolutionaries.
Well-known defensists spoke there on the morning
of the day that I was there, but before my arrival
Alexinsky addressed the congress. There were
fifteen to twenty Social-Democrats among the
teachers, including Bolsheviks and Menshevik-
internationalists; they met separately in a small room
where they exchanged opinions as to the kind of

school they ought to fight for. Many of those present
at that meeting later worked in the district dumas.*
The mass of the teachers were intoxicated with
chauvinism.

I heard both speeches Ilyich delivered on April
4th and his speech at the Petrograd Conference.

On April 18th (May 1st) Ilyich took part in the
May Day demonstration and spoke both on the
Okhta and on the Field of Mars. I did not hear him
as I was so ill that day I could not get up. When
Ilyich returned I was surprised by his excited appearance. When we lived abroad we generally paraded
on May Day, but May Day by police permission is
one thing, and the May Day of the revolutionary
masses, the masses who had triumphed over tsarism,
was different.

On April 21st I had to meet Ilyich at Danskoys. I
had the address, Staro-Nevsky 3, and I walked the
whole length of the Nevsky. A large workers' demonstration came from the Nevsky Gate. Workers
who were crowding on the side-walk greeted the
demonstration. "Let us go," called one young
working woman to another. "Let us go, we will
march all night!" Another crowd wearing hats and
bowlers moved towards the workers' demonstration;
they were greeted by other people with the same
headgear on the sidewalk. The workers predominated nearer the Nevsky Gate, but nearer to Morskaya
Street and Poitseysky Bridge the bowlers and hats
were more numerous. The story was passing from
mouth to mouth among the crowd of how Lenin
had bribed the workers with German gold and now
all were following him. "We must beat Lenin!"
shouted a stylishly dressed girl. "Kill all these
scoundrels," someone in a bowler roared. Class

* Municipal Councils.—Ed.

against Class! The working class stood for Lenin.

From April 24th to the 29th the All-Russian Conference, known as the April Conference, which finally united the Bolsheviks, took place. A hundred and fifty-one delegates attended. A new Central Committee was elected. The questions that were discussed were of extraordinary importance, viz. —the political situation, the war, preparation for organising the Third International, the national question, the agrarian question, and the Party programme.

I remember particularly Ilyich's speech on the political situation.

The most outstanding thing in this speech was the way it clearly revealed Ilyich's attitude to the masses, how closely he observed how the masses lived, and what they thought: "There is no doubt that, as a class, the proletariat and semi-proletariat are not interested in the war. They are influenced by tradition and deception. They still lack political experience. Therefore, our task is that of patiently explaining. Our principles remain intact, we do not make the slightest compromise; yet we cannot approach these masses as we approach the social-chauvinists. These elements of the population have never been Socialists, they have not the slightest conception of Socialism, they are just awakening to political life. But their class-consciousness is growing and broadening with extraordinary rapidity. One must know how to approach them with explanations, and this is now the most difficult task, particularly for a party that but yesterday was underground."*

"Many of us, myself included," said Ilyich in this speech, "have had occasion to address the masses,

* Lenin, *Collected Works*, Vol. XX, Book I, p. 278.

particularly the soldiers, and it seems to me that even when everything is explained to them from the point of view of class interests, there is still one thing in our position that they cannot fully grasp, namely, in what way we intend to finish the war, in what way we think it possible to bring the war to an end. The masses are in a maze of misapprehension, there is an absolute lack of understanding as to our stand, that is why we must be particularly clear in this case."*

". . . . In approaching the masses, we must give concrete answers to all questions."†

"We must be able to carry on the work of explanation," said Ilyich, "not only among the proletariat, but also among wide sections of the petty bourgeoisie."

Speaking of control, Vladimir Ilyich said: "To control, one must have power. If the broad masses of the petty-bourgeois *bloc* do not understand this, we must have the patience to explain it to them, but under no circumstances must we tell them an untruth."‡ Ilyich did not resort to demagogy, and this was felt by the soldiers and peasants who spoke to him. But confidence cannot be won at once. Even in such a time of excitement, Ilyich retained his usual sobriety of thought: "So far we are in the minority; the masses do not trust us yet. We can wait; they will side with us when the government reveals its true nature." Ilyich had many talks with soldiers and peasants and even at that time saw no little evidence of trust, but he had no illusions: "The proletarian party would be guilty of the most grievous error if it shaped its policy on the basis of subjective desires where organisation is required. We cannot assert that the majority is with us; in this

* Lenin, *Collected Works*, Vol. XX, Book I, p. 275.
† *Ibid.*, p. 279.   ‡ *Ibid.*, p. 274.

case our motto should be: caution, caution, caution.
To base our proletarian policy on over-confidence
means to condemn it to failure."*

In concluding his speech on the political situation
Ilyich said: "The Russian Revolution has created the
Soviets. No bourgeois country in the world has or
can have such state institutions. No Socialist revolution can function with any other state power. The
Soviets of Workers' and Soldiers' Deputies must seize
power not for the purpose of building an ordinary,
bourgeois republic, nor for the purpose of introducing Socialism immediately. The latter could not
be accomplished. What, then, is the purpose? They
must seize power in order to take the first concrete
steps towards introducing Socialism, steps that can
and should be taken. In this case fear is the greatest
enemy. The masses should be convinced that these
steps must be taken immediately, that otherwise the
power of the Soviets of Workers' and Soldiers'
Deputies would be devoid of meaning, and would
offer nothing to the people."†

And further, Ilyich spoke of the immediate tasks
before the Soviets. "Private ownership of land must
be abolished. This is our first task, because the majority of the people are for it. To accomplish this
we need the Soviets. This measure cannot be
carried out by means of the old government bureaucracy."‡ And he closed by quoting an example to
illustrate what the struggle for power locally means.
"I shall conclude by referring to the speech that
made the strongest impression on me. I heard a
coal-miner deliver a remarkable speech. Without
using a single bookish word, he told how they had
made the revolution. Those miners were not con-

* Lenin, *Collected Works*, Vol. XX, p. 279.
† *Ibid.*, p. 283.   ‡ *Ibid.*, p. 284.

cerned with the question as to whether or not they should have a president. They seized the mine, and the important question to them was how to keep the cables intact so that production might not be interrupted. Then came the question of bread, of which there was a scarcity. And the miners again agreed on the method of obtaining it. Now this is a real programme of the revolution, not derived from books. This is a real seizure of power locally."*

Zinaida Pavlovna Krzhizhanovskaya once recalled to mind what I told her about the miner in this speech and she said: "Now these miners need engineers mostly. Vladimir Ilyich thinks it would be wonderful if Gleb would go down there."

We met many friends at the Conference. Among others I remember meeting Prisyagin, a student at the Longjumeau school. Listening to Ilyich's speech his eyes glistened. Prisyagin is not alive now, he was killed in the Urals by the Whites in 1918.

At the beginning of May 1917, Ilyich drafted amendments to the Party programme. The imperialist war and the revolution had caused fundamental changes in social life and this required new evaluations and a new approach—the old programme had become obsolete.

The new minimum programme that Ilyich drew up breathed the striving to improve, to raise the standard of living of the masses, a striving to give the masses scope for displaying their initiative.

My work at the secretariat bored me more and more, I wanted to get into real mass work, I also wanted to see Ilyich more often, for I became increasingly anxious about him. The campaign against him was growing in fury. Going down the Petersburg Side, one could hear some housewife

* Lenin, *Collected Works*, Vol. XX, Book I, p. 284.

jeering: "What should be done with this Lenin who came from Germany? Should he be drowned in a well or what?" Of course, the source of these rumours about bribery and treachery was well known, but it was not pleasant to hear. To hear such talk from the bourgeoisie was one thing, but to hear it from the masses was quite another thing. I wrote an article about Lenin for *Soldatskaya Pravda* under the title, "A Page from the History of the Party." Ilyich made some corrections in the manuscript, and it was published in the No. 21 issue, on May 13th, 1917.

Vladimir Ilyich usually returned home tired, and I could not bring myself to question him about affairs. But we both wanted to talk things over as we formerly had on our walks. And sometimes, though rarely, we took walks along the quieter streets on the Petrograd Side. I remember, during one such walk, we were together with Comrades Shauman and Enukidze, and Shauman presented Ilyich with some red badges which his sons had asked him to give to Lenin; Ilyich smiled. Once we strolled with Maria Ilyinishna to one of the islands, but there were such crowds there that we did not get any rest.

I remember Ilyich's speech at the First All-Russian Congress of Soviets of Workers' and Soldiers' Deputies which took place in the Military School on the First Line* on Vasilievsky Island. We passed through a long corridor; the classrooms had been turned into dormitories for the delegates. The hall was crowded. The Bolsheviks sat in a small group at the back of the hall. Although only the Bolsheviks applauded Lenin, there was no doubt about the strong impression his speech created. I do not know

* One of the main streets of Petrograd.—Ed.

how true the story is, but later it was said that as a result of his speech, Kerensky lay unconscious for three hours.

The district Duma elections took place in June. I went to Vasilevsky Island to see what progress was being made in the election campaign. The streets were filled with workers, those from the tube factory predominating. There were many working women from the Lafern factory who had voted for the Socialist-Revolutionaries. Everywhere, groups were engaged in heated argument, but it was not the candidates or the leaders who were being discussed, but the parties, what the various parties were doing, what they stood for. I recalled the municipal elections in Paris; when we were there, we were amazed at the absence of political issues and the volume of personal issues introduced. Here the situation was completely reversed. The development of the masses since 1905-07 was very apparent. It was evident that all read the newspapers of the different political trends. One group was discussing the possibility of Bonapartism. A small, spy-like figure, darting about in the crowd seemed very much out of place in this group of workers who had developed so much in the last few years.

The revolutionary spirit of the masses was growing.

The Bolsheviks had decided to hold a demonstration on June 10th. The Congress prohibited this demonstration and passed a decision to the effect that no demonstrations whatever were to be held for three days. Ilyich then insisted that the demonstration, called by the Petrograd Committee, be abandoned. He argued that since we recognised the power of the Soviets, we were obliged to submit to the decisions of the Congress, otherwise we would be playing into the hands of the enemies. But, yielding to the mood of the masses, the Congress of Soviets itself arranged for a demonstration to be held on June 18th. But the Congress got more than it expected. Nearly four hundred thousand workers and soldiers took part in that demonstration. Ninety per cent. of the banners and placards bore the slogans of the Central Committee of the Bolsheviks: "All power to the Soviets!" "Down with the ten capitalist ministers!" There were only three placards supporting the Provisional government—one of the Bund, the other of the Plekhanov group, *Edinstvo* (*Unity*), and the third of a Cossack regiment. Ilyich characterised June 18th as one of the decisive days. "The demonstration of July 1st (June 18th)," he wrote, "first became a demonstration of the strength and the policies of the revolutionary proletariat which is giving direction to the revolution, and is showing the way out of the blind alley. Therein lies the colossal historical significance of the Sunday demonstration, and therein does it differ in principle from the demonstrations which took place on the day of the funeral of the victims of the revolution, or from those held on May 1st. Then it was a universal tribute to the first victory of the revolution and its heroes, a glance backward, cast by the people over the first lap of the road to freedom and passed by them most quickly and most successfully. The first of May was a holiday of good wishes and hopes bound up with the history of the labour movement of the world, with its ideal of peace and Socialism.

"Neither of the demonstrations aimed at pointing out the direction of the further advance of the revolution. Neither could point out that direction. Neither the first nor the second demonstration had placed before the masses, and in the name of the masses, any concrete and definite questions of the hour, questions as to whither and how the revolution must proceed.

"In this sense the first of July was the first political demonstration of action; it was an exposition of issues not in a book nor in a newspaper, but in the street; not through leaders, but through the masses. It showed how the various classes act, wish to act, and should act, to further the revolution. The bourgeoisie had hidden itself."*

The elections to the district Dumas were over. I was elected to the Vyborg district council. The only candidates to be elected to this council were Bolsheviks and a few Menshevik-Internationalists. The latter, however, did no work on the council. The only ones to work were the Bolsheviks: L. M. Michaelov, Kuchmenko, Chugurin, another comrade and I. At first our council met in the same building as the district Party Committee of which Zhenya Egorova was the secretary, and where Comrade Latsis also worked. Very close contact was maintained between our council and the Party organisation. I learned a great deal from the work in the Vyborg district. It was a good school for Party and Soviet work. During the many years that I had lived abroad as a political exile, I never dared to make a speech even at a small meeting, and until that time I had never written a single line in *Pravda*. I needed such a school very much.

There was a staunch group of active Bolsheviks in the Vyborg district who enjoyed the confidence of the masses of the workers. Soon after I began work on the council, I took over the affairs of the Vyborg district branch of the Committee for the Relief of Soldiers' Wives, of which Nina Alexandrovna Gerd,

* Lenin, *Collected Works*, Vol. XX—"The Revolution of 1917"—Book II, p. 268.—Ed.

the wife of Struve, had been in charge. She was an old friend, we were fellow students at the gymnasium and had taught together at Sunday school.* In the early years of the development of the workers' movement she had been a Social-Democrat. Now we each held entirely different points of view. She gave the work over to me with the remark: "The soldiers' wives do not trust us; they are displeased with whatever we do; they have faith only in the Bolsheviks. Well, you take the work over; perhaps you will be able to do it better than we did." We were not afraid to undertake the work. We were confident that together with the workers, on whose co-operation we could depend, we could develop the work on a wide scale.

The masses of the workers not only took a very active part in politics, but also in educational work. Very soon we set up an Education Council on which there were representatives from all the works and factories of the Vyborg district. I remember that among them were the workers, Puryshev, Kayurov, Yurkin, Gordienko; we met every week and discussed practical measures. When the question came up of the need for introducing general literacy, the workers in all the factories quickly registered all the illiterates. The employers were asked to provide rooms in the factory for classes for instructing the illiterate. When one of them refused, the women workers raised an awful row and exposed the fact that one of the factory rooms was occupied by shock troops (i.e. soldiers selected from particularly chauvinistic battalions). Finally, the employer had to rent premises outside of the factory for the school. A committee of workers was set up to supervise the attendance of the classes and the work of the teachers.

* Workers' educational classes.—Ed.

Near the premises of the district council a machine-gun regiment was stationed. At first this regiment was considered very reliable but its "reliability" quickly disappeared. As soon as it was stationed on the Vyborg Side, agitation began to be carried on among the soldiers. The first to carry on Bolshevik agitation among the soldiers were the sellers of sunflower seeds, kvas,* etc.; many were soldiers' wives. The women workers of the Vyborg district did not resemble those I knew in the 'nineties, or even in the 1905 revolution. They were well dressed, active at meetings and politically intelligent. One woman worker said to me: "My husband is at the front. We lived well together, but I do not know how it will be when he returns. I am for the Bolsheviks now and I will go with them, but I don't know about him there at the front. . . . Does he understand, does he realise that we must follow the Bolsheviks. Often I think at night—perhaps he does not understand and yet. Only I don't know whether I shall see him again, perhaps he will be killed. Yes, and I spit blood, I am going to the hospital." The thin face of this woman worker with the hectic flush on her cheeks, her anxiety about possible difference of opinion with her husband made an indelible impression on my mind. But it was not the working women, but the working men who were most advanced in educational work at that time. The men looked into everything. Comrade Gordienko, for example, was very much occupied with kindergarten work and Comrade Kuklin closely followed the work of the youth.

I also took up work among the youth. A youth league was formed called "Light and Knowledge," and had a programme. The league consisted of

* A kind of cider.—Ed.

Bolsheviks, Mensheviks, Anarchists and adherents of
no party. The programme was most naïve and
primitive, but the arguments that arose around it
were very interesting. For instance, one of the items
was that all members must learn to sew. Then one
young fellow, a Bolshevik, asked: "Why should everyone learn to sew? Girls, of course, must be able to
sew, otherwise, later on, they will not be able to sew
buttons on their husbands' trousers, but why should
all learn?" These words raised a storm of indignation. Not only the girls but everybody expressed
indignation and jumped up from their seats. "The
wife must sew buttons on trousers? What do you
mean? Do you want to uphold the old slavery of
women? The wife is her husband's comrade, not
his servant!" The lad who proposed that only
women learn to sew had to surrender. I remember
a conversation with another lad, Murashev by name,
an ardent supporter of the Bolsheviks. I asked him:
"Why don't you join the Bolshevik Party?" "You
see," he answered, "several of us young people
joined the Party. But why did we join? Do you
think because we understood that the Bolsheviks
were right? Not for that reason, but because the
Bolsheviks distributed revolvers! That's no good.
When one joins a Party one must know what it
stands for. I returned my card until I should fully
understand." It must be said that only the revolutionary-minded young men and women joined the
"Light and Knowledge" League; they would not
tolerate anyone in their midst who expressed con-
servative views. The members were very active,
spoke at meetings at their factories, and at their own
meetings. But they were very trustful. This trust-
fulness had to be combatted.

I had quite a lot of work to do among the women.

I had already got over my former shyness and spoke wherever it was necessary.

I plunged right into the work. I wanted to draw the masses into social work, to do the utmost to make it possible to establish that "people's militia" of which Lenin had spoken.

After I started work in the Vyborg district, I saw still less of Ilyich, but times were becoming acute, the struggle was blazing forth. June 18th was remarkable, not only for the demonstration of four hundred thousand workers and soldiers that took place under Bolshevik slogans; on that day the Provisional government, after vacillating for months, submitted to the pressure of the Allies and started the offensive at the front. The Bolsheviks had already started to agitate in the press and at meetings. The Provisional government felt that the ground was slipping from under its feet. On June 28th the news of the first defeats of the Russian army at the front was received; this excited the soldiers very much.

At the end of June Ilyich, accompanied by Maria Ilyinishna, went to visit Bonch-Bruevich, who lived in the village of Neyvola, near Mustamyaki (not far from Petrograd), to take a few days' rest. While they were away the following incident occurred in Petrograd. The machine-gun regiment stationed on the Vyborg Side decided to start an armed uprising. Two days before this our education committee had arranged to meet the education committee of the regiment on Monday to discuss certain educational questions. Of course, no one came from the regiment. The whole regiment had gone. On my way to the Kshesinsky Palace I saw the machine-gun soldiers on Samsonevsky Avenue marching in good order. The following scene impressed itself on my memory: an old worker stepped off the side-walk, walked towards the marching soldiers and, bowing low, said loudly: "Now, brothers, do stand up for the working people." Among those who were present at the headquarters of the Central Committee in the Kshesinsky Palace were Comrades Stalin and Lashevich. The machine-gun regiment marched to the palace. When they got there they halted near the balcony, saluted and then marched on. Later, two more regiments marched to the headquarters of the Central Committee, then a workers' demonstration came. In the evening a comrade was sent to Mustamyaki for Ilyich. The Central Committee had issued the slogan to turn the demonstration into a peaceful one, but the machine-gun regiment was already erecting barricades. I can recall Comrade Lashevich, who led the work in this regiment, lying for a long time on a couch in a room at the Vyborg council, looking at the ceiling, reluctant to go to the machine-gunners to stop them. It was hard for him to go, but such was the decision of the Central Committee. The works and factories were on strike. Sailors had arrived from Kronstadt. A huge demonstration of armed workers and soldiers was marching to the Taurida Palace. Ilyich spoke from the balcony of the Kshesinsky Palace. The Central Committee issued a manifesto for a cessation of the demonstration. The Provisional government called out the Junkers* and Cossacks, who opened fire on the demonstrators at Sadovaya Street. It was arranged that Ilyich pass that night at the Sulimovs (on the Petersburg Side), but it was safest for him to hide on the Vyborg Side. It was decided that he would live at the house of Kayurov, a worker. I went to Sulimovs to inform Ilyich of the arrangement and we both went to the Vyborg Side. We

* Students of the military school.—Ed.

passed the Moscow Regiment marching along a boulevard, Kayurov was sitting in the boulevard, and seeing us, he walked ahead and Ilyich followed him. I turned back. The Junkers completely wrecked the editorial office of *Pravda*. During the day a meeting of the Petrograd Committee was held in the watchman's room at the Reno factory, at which Ilyich was present. The question of a general strike was discussed and it was decided not to call the strike. From there Ilyich went to the apartment of Comrade Fofanova in Lesnoye, where he met several of the members of the Central Committee. That day the workers' movement was suppressed. Alexinsky, a former representative of the Petrograd workers in the Second Duma, a *Vperyod*-ist, who at one time had been a close associate in our work, and Pankratov, a member of the Socialist-Revolutionary Party and an old Schluesselberg prisoner, issued a slanderous statement to the effect that they had authentic information that Lenin was a German spy. They believed that this slander would paralyse Lenin's influence. On July 6th, the Provisional government issued an order for the arrest of Lenin, Zinoviev and Kamenev. The Kshesinsky Palace was occupied by government troops. Lenin left Kayurov's house to go to Alliluevs where Zinoviev was also in hiding, as Kayurov's son was an anarchist; the young men were playing around with bombs and the house was not very safe for hiding.

On the 7th, Maria Ilyinishna and I went to visit Ilyich at Alliluev's house. This was just the moment when Ilyich wavered. He argued that he ought to surrender to the authorities and appear in court. Maria Ilyinishna objected violently. "Gregory and I have decided to appear, go and tell Kamenev," Ilyich said to me. At that time Kamenev was staying

nearby at another flat. I hastily made ready to go.
"Let us say good-bye," Vladimir Ilyich said, stopping
me—"we may not see each other again," we em-
braced. I went to Kamenev and delivered Vladimir
Ilyich's message. In the evening, Comrade Stalin
and others urged Ilyich not to appear in Court
and finally convinced him; by that they saved his
life. That evening the military raided our flat on
Shirokaya Street. A colonel and another military
man in a grey coat with a white lining appeared.
They searched only our room and took some notes
and my documents from the table. They asked me if
I knew where Ilyich was, and from this I concluded
that he had not given himself up. In the morning I
went to Comrade Smilga, who also lived on Shirokaya Street; Stalin and Molotov lived with him.
I learned from them that Ilyich and Zinoviev had
decided to hide.

Two days later, on the 9th, a horde of Junkers
raided the house and ransacked the whole flat.
Mark Timofeyevich Elizarov, the husband of Anna
Ilyinishna, was in the house and they thought he was
Ilyich. They questioned me about Ilyich. At that
time the Elizarovs had a servant, Annushka, a girl
who came from a remote village and knew nothing
about what was going on. She was very anxious to
learn to read and write and at every spare moment
she read her primer, but she was a poor scholar:
"I am a village blockhead," she sorrowfully exclaimed. I tried to help her learn to read and understand something about the various parties, the war,
etc. She had no idea who Lenin was. I was not
home on the 8th; our people told me afterwards that
an automobile drove up to the house and that a
hostile demonstration was made. Suddenly Annushka ran in and yelled: "Some sort of Olenins have

arrived." During the search, the Junkers began to question her and, pointing to Mark Timofeyevich, they asked his name. She did not know. They decided that she did not want to tell. They then searched the kitchen, even looking under her bed. Annushka indignantly remarked: "Look in the oven, someone may be sitting there." They took the three of us, Mark Timofeyevich, Annushka and me, to the General Staff Headquarters. There they put us at some distance from each other, an armed soldier at the side of each. After a while, some officers burst in in a rage, ready to throw themselves at us. But the colonel who had been in charge of the first search came in, looked at us and said: "These are not the people we want." Had Ilyich been there, they would have torn him to pieces. We were dismissed. Mark Timofeyevich insisted that they give us an automobile to go home in. The colonel promised and left, but of course we were not given an automobile. We hired a cab. The bridges were drawn up, so we did not reach home until morning. We knocked at the door a long time and were beginning to fear that something had happened to our people, but finally the door was opened.

Our place was searched a third time when I was away at the district council. I came home and found the entrance occupied by soldiers and the street full of people. I remained there a while and then went back to the district council without going in as, in any case, I could not have been of any assistance. When I reached the district council, it was already late, no one was there but the caretaker. Shortly, Slutsky, a comrade who had recently arrived from America, arrived together with Volodarsky, Melnichansky and others; Slutsky was later killed on the southern front. He had just been under arrest and

urged me not to go home, but to send someone in the
morning to find out what had happened. We went
out to look for a place to spend the night, but we
did not know the addresses of comrades. We wandered through the district a long time before we
came upon Fofanova, a comrade who worked in the
district, who put us up for the night. In the morning
we found that none of our people had been arrested
and that this time the search had not been as rough
as the preceding ones.

Ilyich and Zinoviev were in hiding at the house of
an old member of the underground Party organisation, Emelyanov, who worked at the Sestroretsk
factory and lived at Razliv, near Sestroretsk. Ilyich
always retained a warm feeling towards Emelyanov
and his family.

I spent all my time in the Vyborg district. During
the July days I was struck with the difference between the spirit of the petty bourgeoisie and that of
the workers. On the trams, in the streets, from all
corners could be heard the mutterings of discontent,
but across the wooden bridge on the Vyborg Side
one came upon an entirely different world. There
were many things to do. Through Comrade Zoft
and others connected with Comrade Emelyanov, I
received various messages from Ilyich. The reaction
increased. On July 9th the joint meeting of the All-
Russian Central Executive Committee and the
Executive Committee of the Soviet of Workers' and
Peasants' Deputies declared the Provisional government to be "the government of salvation of the
revolution"; on the same day the "salvation" began.
On that day Kamenev was arrested; on July 12th
the order was given for the introduction of capital
punishment at the front; on July 15th, *Pravda* and
Okopnaya Pravda (*Trench Truth*) were suppressed, and

an order was issued prohibiting meetings at the front. Bolsheviks were arrested in Helsingfors, and *Volna*, the Bolshevik newspaper there, was suppressed. On July 18th the Finnish Diet was dissolved, General Kornilov was appointed Commander-in-Chief, on July 22nd Trotsky and Lunacharsky were arrested.

Soon after the July days, Kerensky devised a scheme by which he thought army discipline would be raised; he decided to march the machine-gun regiment which had started the demonstration in the July days, unarmed, into a public square and there degrade them. I saw the disarmed regiment march into the square. As they led their horses by the bridle so much hatred burned in their eyes, there was so much hatred expressed in their slow march, that it was clear that a more stupid method could not have been devised. And as a matter of fact, in October, the machine-gun regiment followed the Bolsheviks to a man, the machine gunners guarding Ilyich at Smolny.

The Bolshevik Party was reduced to semi-legality; but it grew in numbers and strength. By the time the VI Congress of the Party was opened, on July 26th, the membership had reached one hundred and seventy-seven thousand, twice as large as it was three months previously at the All-Russian Bolshevik Conference. There could be no doubt of the growth of Bolshevik influence, particularly in the army. The VI Party Congress helped still further to rally the forces of the Bolsheviks. The Congress issued a manifesto in which it called attention to the counter-revolutionary position taken by the Provisional government. "The world revolution and the battle of classes are impending," the manifesto stated. "Our Party is entering this battle with its banner unfurled. It has firmly held this banner in its grasp. It has not dropped it before the violators and slanderers, before traitors to the revolution and flunkeys of capital. It will hold the banner aloft in the struggle for Socialism, for the brotherhood of nations, for it knows—that a new movement is rising and that the death hour of the old world is approaching."

On August 25th, Kornilov with his troops began to march on Petrograd. The Petrograd workers and the Vyborg workers were the first, of course, to rush to the defence of Petrograd. Our agitators were sent to encounter the first detachments of Kornilov's troops, the "wild division" as they were called. The Kornilov forces were quickly disintegrated and no real fighting took place. General Krymov, the commander of the corps which was to attack Petrograd, shot himself. I recall the figure of one of our Vyborg workers, a young fellow who worked on our educational committee, running into the district Duma with a rifle still on his shoulder. He had just returned from the front where he was among the first to go. Although when he entered his face was still flushed with the excitement of battle, he threw his rifle into a corner and began to talk heatedly about crayons, of which there was a shortage at the school, and about blackboards. Every day I had the opportunity to observe how closely the workers in the Vyborg district linked the revolutionary struggle with the struggle for mastering knowledge and culture.

It was no longer possible for Ilyich to continue living in the hut near Razliv, where he was in hiding. The autumn came and Ilyich decided to cross over to Finland. He wished to work on his book *State and Revolution*, for which he had collected a considerable amount of material, and which he had already thought out and planned. In Finland it was also more convenient to follow the newspapers.

N. A. Emelyanov obtained a passport belonging to a Sestroretsk workman and Ilyich put on a wig and made up to resemble this workman. Dimitry Ilyich Leschenko, at whose house Lenin had often slept, went to Razliv to photograph Ilyich for the passport (a photograph had to be affixed to the passport). Comrade Leschenko was an old Party comrade of 1905-1907, who had formerly been associate editor of our Bolshevik paper and who at the time was helping me in educational work in the Vyborg district. A Finnish comrade, Yalava, an engine-driver on the Finnish Railway, whom Comrades Shotman and Rakhya knew well, undertook to get Ilyich across, disguised as a fireman. The plan succeeded. All connections with Ilyich were also maintained through Comrade Yalava and on more than one occasion I went to Comrade Yalava, who lived in the Vyborg district, for letters from Ilyich. After Ilyich was settled in Helsingfors, he sent a letter written in invisible ink asking me to come; he sent his address and even drew a map with directions to his place so that I might not have to ask anyone how to reach it. But I scorched the edge of the map when I heated the letter over the lamp. The Emelyanovs obtained for me a passport belonging to an old Sestroretsk working woman, and I covered my head with a shawl and went to Razliv to meet them. They accompanied me across the border. All that was required of persons living in that locality was a permit to cross the border. An officer glanced at my permit. I had to walk five versts through a forest from the border to Olilla, a small station, where I took a soldiers' train. Everything went off well, except for a delay caused by the lack of directions

contained on that part of the map which I had
burned. I wandered through the streets a long time
until I found the street I wanted. Ilyich was very
glad to see me. The effects of living in seclusion when
it was so necessary for him to be in the midst of the
preparation for battle were apparent. I stayed in
Helsingfors for a couple of days and told him all the
news. When I left, Ilyich escorted me to the last
turn of the road, although he wanted very much to
accompany me to the station. We arranged that I
should come again.

Two weeks later I again visited Ilyich. I was de-
layed for some reason and decided not to go to the
Emelyanovs but to go straight to Olilla by myself.
When I reached the forest night began to fall—it
was already mid-autumn—the moon rose. My feet
began to sink in the sand. It seemed to me that I
had lost the road; I hurried on. Finally I reached
Olilla but I had to wait half an hour for the train.
The train was filled with soldiers and sailors and was
so crowded that I had to stand all the way. The
soldiers openly spoke of an uprising; the only thing
they talked about was politics. The scene in the car
was like that at an extremely exciting meeting. None
but soldiers and sailors were in the car. One civilian
did come in at first, but after listening to the soldiers
relating how they threw officers into the river, he got
out as quickly as he could at the next station. No
one paid any attention to me. When I told Ilyich
what they talked about, his face became thoughtful
and remained so no matter what he talked of. It
was apparent that his mind was not on what he was
saying, it was fixed on rebellion and how best to
prepare for it.

On September 13th-14th Ilyich wrote the letter
Marxism and Rebellion to the Central Committee; at

the end of September he left Helsingfors for Vyborg, so as to be nearer to Petrograd. From Vyborg he wrote to Smilga in Helsingfors (Smilga was at that time the chairman of the regional committee of the army, navy and workers of Finland), that all attention must be devoted to the preparation of the Finnish army and navy for war to overthrow Kerensky. His mind was constantly engaged on the problem of how to reorganise the whole state apparatus, how the masses were to be reorganised, how the whole social "fabric" was to be rewoven— as he expressed it. He wrote about this in his article, "Will the Bolsheviks Retain Power?" He wrote about this in his manifesto to the peasants and soldiers, in a letter he sent to the Petrograd City Conference to be read at a private meeting where concrete measures to be taken for the seizure of power were being discussed; he wrote about this to the members of the Central Committee, the Petrograd Committee, the Moscow Committee, and the Bolshevik members of the Petrograd and Moscow Soviets.

On October 7th Ilyich moved from Vyborg to Petrograd. It was decided to maintain strict secrecy concerning his whereabouts; not even to inform the Central Committee of his address. We housed him on the Vyborg Side at the flat of Marguerita Vasilyevna Fofanovna, which was in a large house at the corner of Lesnoy Avenue, almost entirely inhabited by workers. The apartment was very suitable for the purpose, for most of the family had left in the summer and had not yet returned, even the servants, and Marguerita Vasilyevna was an ardent Bolshevik. She carried out all Ilyich's errands. Three days later, on October 10th, Ilyich attended a meeting of the Central Committee at Suchanov's

flat, where a resolution in favour of an armed insur-
rection was passed. Ten members of the Central
Committee voted in favour of the resolution—Lenin,
Sverdlov, Stalin, Dzerzhinsky, Trotsky, Uritsky,
Kollontai, Bubnov, Sokolnikov and Lomov. Zino-
viev and Kamenev voted against it.

On October 15th a meeting of the Petrograd
organisation took place at the Smolny Institute (this
fact alone was very significant); district delegates
were present (eight from the Vyborg district). I
remember Dzerzhinsky speaking in favour of an
armed insurrection. Chudnovsky spoke against it.
Chudnovsky's arm was bandaged, he had been
wounded at the front. Excitedly, he pointed out
that defeat was inevitable, that we must not hurry.
"Nothing is easier than to die for the revolution, but
we will jeopardise the revolution if we just allow
ourselves to be shot." Chudnovsky actually did die
for the revolution; he was killed during the civil war.
He was not a phrase-monger, but his point of view
was thoroughly wrong. I do not remember the
other speeches. When the vote was taken the overwhelming majority was found to be in favour of
immediate insurrection. All the Vyborg delegates
voted for it.

Next day, the 16th, an enlarged meeting of the
Central Committee was held in the premises of the
Lesnoe sub-district Duma on Lesnaya Street, at
which, in addition to the members of the Central
Committee, there were present members of the Executive Committee of the Petrograd Committee, the
military organisation, the Petrograd Council of
Trade Unions, members of the factory and works
committees, and of the Petrograd District Committee
of the railroad workers. At this meeting there were
two fractions, the majority which was in favour of

immediate insurrection, and the minority, which was against it. Lenin's resolution was carried by an overwhelming majority, nineteen for, two against and four abstaining. The question was decided. At a private meeting of the Central Committee, a military revolutionary centre was elected. Very few came to see Lenin—I, Maria Ilyinishna and sometimes Comrade Rakhya. I recollect the following scene. Ilyich had sent Fofanovna on some errand; it was arranged that he would not open the door for anyone and that he would not respond to the bell. It was also arranged that I knock in a certain manner. Fofanovna had a cousin who attended a military school. I came in the evening and saw this fellow on the staircase. He appeared embarrassed. He saw me and said: "Someone has stolen into Marguerita's apartment." "What do you mean, stolen in?" "Yes, I came, rang and a man's voice answered. Then I rang and rang and nobody answered." I told him a tale about Marguerita having gone to a meeting, and that I was sure he was mistaken about hearing the voice. I only felt at ease when he left and boarded a tram. I then turned back and knocked in the manner agreed upon. When Ilyich opened the door, I began to scold him: "The fellow might have called other people," I said. "I thought it was something urgent," Ilyich replied in excuse. I, too, was carrying Ilyich's messages most of the time. On October 24th he wrote to the Central Committee urging the necessity of taking power that day. He sent Marguerita with this message. But not waiting for her return, he put on a wig and went to the Smolny himself. Not a minute was to be lost. He met Marguerita on the way and told her he was going to the Smolny and that she need not wait for him.

The Vyborg district was preparing for the insurrection. There were fifty women workers in the premises of the Vyborg Council during the entire night, a woman doctor was giving them instructions in first aid. In the rooms of the district committee the workers were being armed; group after group came to the committee and received rifles and ammunition. But in the Vyborg district there was no one to be suppressed—they arrested only a colonel and a few Junkers who had come into a workers' club to have some tea. In the evening Zhenya Egorova and I went to the Smolny on a truck to find out how things were going.

On October 25th (November 7th), 1917, the Provisional government was overthrown. Political power passed to the Military Revolutionary Committee—the organ of the Petrograd Soviet which stood at the head of the Petrograd proletariat and garrison. On the same day, the Military Revolutionary Council transferred power to the Second All-Russian Congress of the Soviet of Workers' and Soldiers' Deputies. A workers' and peasants' government was formed, a Council of People's Commissars was set up, the chairman of which was Lenin.